A Different Drummer

The Escapades of a Ten-Pound Pom

(a sortamemoir)

Nigel Ridgway

A catalogue record for this book is available from the National Library of Australia

Copyright © 2020 Nigel Ridgway
All rights reserved.
ISBN-13: 978-1-922343-47-5

Linellen Press
265 Boomerang Road
Oldbury, Western Australia
www.linellenpress.com.au

Dedication

This book is dedicated to:
    My daughter Samantha, and my grandsons 'T', 'B' and 'D'
    My patient wife Aileen and my great Aussie family
    Musician friends (both rock 'n' roll and jazz) who give much of their lives entertaining others.
    Sailing friends and their enduring friendship – they know the sea in all its moods and still love her!

Contents

Dedication iii

Contents v

Acknowledgments vii

Chapter One - Being a Baby Boomer 1

Chapter Two - Some Family History 11

Chapter Three - Off to the Middle East – Jordan 30

Chapter Four - Musical Awakenings 37

Chapter Five - Working Life 64

Chapter Six - Sailing Years 78

Chapter Seven - Emigrating to Australia 99

Chapter Eight - Marriage and Children 107

Chapter Nine - Losing a Child 116

Chapter Ten - Obara's Arrest, Trial and Sentencing 122

Chapter Eleven - Happier Times 125

Chapter Twelve - Musings in The Time of Corona 134

   Some of my favourite reads *148*

About the Author 150

Acknowledgements

Huge thanks to my friend Jan Thompson for her patience proof-reading and editing; excellent work.
To Pauline Yarwood, retired journalist, for suggestions and advice.
Many thanks to my wife, Aileen, for her assistance on the computer and her patience.
To the guys at Minuteman Press in Balcatta, Simon and Fernando – thanks for your help.
To Helen Iles at Linellen Press for accepting my manuscript for publication and for her expert advice and enthusiasm.

Chapter One

Being a Baby Boomer

"We're here for a good time, not a long time!"
Baby Boomers' Credo

"Bloody hell, Ridgway, no bird is worth this! You stupid bugger!"

That's what I was telling myself as I hung on for dear life on the buffers between two passenger carriages on a train from Gothenberg to Orebro in Sweden. I was on a mission to meet up with an exchange student, a beautiful Swedish brunette named Margarita who had been staying in our village in Suffolk, England. How the hell did I end up on the buffers? Well, I'd been sprung by the conductor on the train. I'd nipped aboard in Gothenberg, found a seat and slung my little backpack in the baggage area. The carriage was not overcrowded and I had a good view along it to look out for the ticket inspector. I had very little money so hoped to get a ride for gratis. An hour or so into the journey, I saw the inspector open the inter-joining door between carriages and begin to check tickets. While his back was turned, I sneaked into the toilet, hiding right behind the door making myself as small as possible. All was good for a while, then the door opened and someone came in. The door was pressed up against me but the train lurched and it sprung shut. It was the bloody inspector! He'd come into the toilet to wash his hands. I muttered something – he just marched me to a seat and told me (in English) to stay there until the next station. As I couldn't produce a ticket he said I'd have to see the stationmaster when the train stopped.

As the train slowed into the next station, I jumped off and, once it stopped completely, dived between the carriages, climbing up on the buffers on the other side. I grabbed the handrails above and just hung on. I could hear some yelling in Swedish on the platform side but soon the train pulled out. So there I was, nineteen years of age, trying to get to see a Swedish girl I'd fallen for, hanging onto the outside of a train travelling at quite a speed through the Swedish countryside! Mad bastard! One slip and I'd have gone onto the track and been strawberry jam. It was not that cold, being September, but I was almost frozen by the time we reached Orebro. Unfortunately, the platform for Orebro was on the same side as I was this time – you should have seen the look of horror and amazement on the faces of the people waiting to get on! I must have looked like JC on the cross. As the train stopped, I jumped off, ducked back into the carriage to grab my backpack and sauntered down the platform. I sat on a seat and waited until the train pulled out. The station was deserted so I just wandered out and looked for a bus. I got away with it.

Did I find my lovely Swedish girl? You'll have to read on …

*****

Those of us fortunate enough to be included in the baby boomer demographic are, to my mind, the luckiest generation to have ever lived on this planet. We've had it all. Most of us never had to go to war (Vietnam excluded); our music was remarkable; we challenged the establishment of our time; we experimented with drugs, sex and relationships; we had incredible freedom; we always found work; we saw the introduction of amazing technology; we could afford to buy our own homes and, to cap it all off, we had a bloody good time.

We get a lot of flak from the younger generations but we were just fortunate to be born at that particular time in history so we don't really need to apologise for being a Boomer – it wasn't our fault. Our catch cry was, "I'm here for a good time, not a long time!" And then COVID-19 hit us in our 70s – what a great leveller. How we handled it and survived – or not – I'll bring up in the final chapter.

Never has a generation experienced and experimented so much. We were so different from our parents' generation which was frugal and bound by middle-class values. But then we hadn't fought a world war. I remember that my childhood in England just after the war was filled with the romanticism of it all – Spitfires and Hurricanes taking off from green English fields to shoot down those nasty Germans in their Stukas, Messerschmidts and Heinkels. I made balsa wood and tissue models of those famous World War II fighters and flew them across England's green and pleasant land – completely oblivious to the reality of war. My room as a kid was filled with plastic and balsa/tissue models of many planes, ships, tanks and guns – I had them hanging from the ceiling, on shelves and all over any space I could find.(As a granddad, I have some hanging up now!)

My favourite model was of an aircraft carrier. It had hundreds of plastic pieces and took me many months to complete. Another one I loved was a free-flight balsa plane that was driven by a 1hp diesel engine. To start the thing, you screwed down the compression screw as hard as you could then flicked over the prop with your fingers. After a few flicks and a bit of smoke, the engine roared into life and then you launched the plane by hand – and it would fly right up high, in a big turn (the rudder was set at an angle) and then glide back to earth when the motor ran out of fuel (the fuel was ether). Great fun for a boy and I had many hours of pleasure flying that plane.

Bonfire night – or Guy Fawkes Night – November 5th was always a bit dangerous. We'd fire rockets at each other and see how long you could hold a banger in your hand before it exploded. No wonder kids got lots of injuries. Small boys love explosions! I used to put a banger in one of my balsa/tissue rubber-powered planes, light the fuse, then launch it from my upstairs bedroom window. It was wonderful to hear the banger go off with a loud *bang!* then envelope the plane in flames as it crashed into the ground. Small boys can be destructive and horrible … …

Another crazy thing we did was to scrape the ends off matchsticks, get hold of two bolts and a nut and stuff the highly flammable powder into the nut. Then we'd screw the bolts into the nut as tightly as we could. We'd find some bitumen or concrete and hurl the thing onto the ground as hard as we could. So dangerous – the contraption exploded and the missile could go in any direction, just like a bullet. Luckily no-one I knew was hurt.

My father and step-father never spoke of the war until I was in my forties. My friends and I only knew what was served up in comics and adventure books when we were kids. The Germans were always depicted as slightly stupid 'Square Heads' and our forces as good-looking, lantern-jawed heroes, calling out, "Tally Ho, Green Leader, bandits at 11 o'clock!" before they attacked in their Spitfires. It wasn't until much later in life that I understood there were such things as propaganda from both sides. I think many boys of my age really wanted the war experience and felt we had missed out on testing our 'manhoods'.

Incidentally, I did try to show students the 'Battle of Britain' movie at various times when I was teaching but they were not interested at all. They could not relate to pilots scrambling to take off in time to intercept the enemy; it was just not possible in their eyes. This is also true of the moon landing in 1969 – some kids just don't believe it could have happened and think it was all staged in a film studio just to beat the Russians.

*****

So who, exactly, qualifies to be a baby boomer? The official demographic says it's the babies born after the Second World War from 1946 until 1961. I was actually born a bit early, as I was born late December 1945, but I have always considered myself to be a boomer since I learned of the term. I was a 'blue baby' so I guess I'm lucky to be here at all.

I always sensed there was some huge difference between myself and my parents. I loved them but found their world very stuffy and conventional. We were always having to mind our 'p's and q's' – try explaining that to today's kids! Manners were expected and enforced, including the way we ate and held our knives and forks. Dress standards were seen to be important, especially if visiting or being visited. In our family, I think we were quite Victorian as my mother always used to say, "Children should be seen and not heard."

Both my parents had very 'posh' accents, as did the rest of the family, but I didn't inherit one.

Visiting rellies was a bit starchy for my brother and me. After the formalities of introductions, we couldn't wait to escape and play outside. To this day, I still find 'rellie do's' a bit awkward.

Mother was not all that hard on us kids most of the time and she had a wonderful sense of humour. There was always lots of laughter at home and my mum would 'laugh like a drain' – as she put it – at funny incidences, like the time her knickers fell down in public in front of some soldiers!

My mum Deirdre and stepdad Charles

Childhood was fun as we could pretty well please ourselves what we did as long as we were home in time for dinner. We were always making things like billy-carts, modifying and painting our bikes, playing with cap guns and fireworks and out exploring the neighbourhood.

We would cycle for miles to find rivers and woods where we could construct cubby houses and dens. My stepdad was in the RAF and we moved around the UK a lot. Most of his postings were in country towns and villages in England so there were always plenty of new places to explore. Some of the villages and towns of my childhood I recall were Sandwich in Kent, Nether Wallop in Hampshire (that village was part of a trio: Nether Wallop, Middle Wallop and Over Wallop – can you believe those names?) Andover (Hampshire), Shepton Mallet in Somerset, Ashley Heath (Hampshire), Hull in Yorkshire and Alderton in Suffolk. I was actually born in Wincanton, Somerset. Germany and Jordan in the Middle East were postings added to the list. All that moving meant making new friends and probably gave me the typical Boomers' itchy-feet, eventually causing me to migrate to Australia in 1966.

The little village of Nether Wallop was very picturesque and we rented a thatched cottage there. A small river ran through the middle of the village and we could catch little stickle-backs and the occasional trout. Charles, my stepdad, worked at RAF Middlle Wallop, not far away. I liked to cycle there and watch Austers and Ballios (RAF training aircraft) take off and land, doing circuits and bumps with novice pilots at the controls. Middle Wallop had gained a good reputation during the Battle of Britain.

One day, Mike and I found this baby jackdaw (a member of the crow family) after he'd fallen out of his nest. We nursed him and brought him up and he became a family pet. He could talk a bit and was very cheeky. He used to fly down to the bus stop where we caught the bus to school (another school – St Probus in Salisbury – but at least it was a day school!) and meet me at

the end of the day. He would sit on my head or shoulder as I rode my bike home! We loved him but one day he disappeared. We think he was nicked, as talking jackdaws could be quite valuable. We searched and searched but never saw him again. He was never caged and always sat in trees near the cottage, or came down when he wanted company and some food.

Mike and I ready for day school in Salisbury

I don't remember that much about my very early days. My mum used to tell me that I was a lovely little boy because I could amuse myself for many hours and didn't demand constant attention, unlike my brother Mike. I recall turning big cardboard boxes into cars or the cockpit of an aeroplane and making the appropriate noises! Later, of course, I loved making models and still do in retirement. Kindy was fun. My mother remembers me going through the other kid's satchels looking for snacks – I was always hungry. The headmistress was not that amused but I didn't get into too much trouble.

Mike and I were quite close as little boys but once he was sent off to boarding school, we drifted apart. Middle-class families of that era seemed to deem it mandatory for boys to go to boarding school.

As little boys with Deirdre

My parents were tolerant in many ways. I was never expected to attend church or Sunday school and my mother always referred to herself as an agnostic. I don't think religion, politics or sex were ever discussed at the dinner table, though. Years later, when I read George Bernard Shaw who wrote that, "All intelligent men (and I presume women too) are interested in politics, religion and sex" I fell about laughing as I remembered our rather stilted dinner conversations.

As I reached my teens my mother used to ask me what I'd like to do with my life and I would say, "I want to experience as much as I can!" She never scolded me for that – but she would if I'd dared to lick my plate after a good meal. And I did experience so much.

They were magic years growing up with so much personal freedom. I think of the way many mums molly-coddle their kids today (helicopter parents were just not around back then) and I squirm. We were allowed to learn by our mistakes, even if we made them over and over again. I understand the world has changed and our casual childhood is a thing of the past. Having to make your own fun made us less dependent on our parents for stimulation but perhaps we may not have been as close to them as today's kids are to their parents?

My dear parents, little did they know that we were going to challenge all they stood for and that their conservative world was going to change forever. In my teens, late teens and twenties I drifted so far away from my parents and their values that the gap was never bridged for many, many years – nineteen years in fact, when I returned to England from Australia to see them. By then I had accepted many of their values and had become an almost 'respectable' son.

Are we Boomers a self-indulgent, hedonistic, selfish lot? I don't think we are – we worked bloody hard. Not that I'm suggesting that all Boomers lived the life I lived but we did have the opportunity to do so many things that were different from the parental expectations of the previous generation. Many of my friends and acquaintances lived perfectly 'normal' suburban lives and stayed in the one career and marriage all their lives – and often in the same town or village. The combination of my own curiosity about the world and society and my own restless upbringing is what drove me try so many different experiences.

Not that I became famous or highly successful at anything. I always seemed to be on the peripheral of big changes and events, more of a spectator at times than a participant. I never made lots of money but always seemed to have enough. I wasn't particularly ambitious. Most of my school reports usually said, "Could do better if he tried." Of course *anyone* can do better if they try and I always thought it an amusing comment. There have been so many books about people overcoming some awful personal illness like cancer or depression, that I'm hoping my mainly light-hearted story will add a bit of humour and fun. I've had my share of tragedy too and have experienced the 'black dog' but have learned to live with it. Above all, I'd like to write honestly and simply. We all have a story to tell – but it's not so easy to put it in writing at times. The blank page staring at you can be quite daunting! Here we are clinging to life on a blue and white ball spinning around in space, just the right distance from our sun to sustain life – even as a little boy, I remember thinking, "What's this all about?"

Chapter Two

Some Family History

"Other things may change us, but we start and end with the family"   Anthony Brandt

The trauma of constant moving for a little boy can be quite profound. I don't suppose my parents ever thought about it, as it was the norm in the services. All my family had been in the services. Grandfather, on my mother's side, a Scot, Charles Plowman Murchie, was a pilot in the Great War, flying SE5a biplanes for the fledgling RFC (Royal Flying Corps). How I would have loved to hear about his war experiences. He wrote a book but I could never find a copy. He was a 'distant' granddad and I only remember him vaguely. I used to call him Daddygran. In World War II, he joined up again as an army captain and became involved with MI9. He helped many downed pilots escape back to Britain through Spain, working with the French Resistance – very dangerous work and I would love to have read his book.

One quirky thing my mum remembered about his experiences was that he insisted his rescued pilots and soldiers all ate raw onions to ward off germs and colds. His third wife, Rita, was Italian and they ended up on the Isle of Elba, so maybe that's why no one could find a copy of his book. He was only 66 when he died. A lesson for families – someone should take charge of its history and retain any writings or diaries. Once gone, it's gone forever unless you can find it on Google.

Daddygran (grandad) was proud of his RFC wings

Grandfather on my father's side was a seaman on Q ships in WWI. These were merchant ships converted to warships with the addition of guns that were hidden behind steel panels. When approaching a ship, the panels would be dropped and then they opened fire – a bit sneaky! Their main purpose was to lure submarines to the surface so they could be fired upon. My father, Denis Woolnough Mills, went on to join the Royal Navy as a career officer in 1937, entering Dartmouth as a midshipman. A midshipman is called a 'Snotty' in the navy. He commanded submarines in the Second World War and won a DSC for his part in landing frogmen in midget subs (chariots) on the shores of Italy to blow up Italian warships. He was first lieutenant (2IC) on *HMS Thunderbolt* in 1943 for the Italian raid. His first command was *HMS Seawolf* from August 1943 until August 1944.

HMS Seawolf, 1944. My father, Lt Cdr D.W. Mills was skipper

He and my mother divorced just after the war so I never knew about this story until I met him when I was in my forties. When we finally met, it was as if I'd always known him and we became firm friends. He was Commanding Officer on seven subs, one of which he sailed to Australia. He ran aground somewhere on the Barrier Reef and was stranded until high tide. This almost cost him his command but his No 2 was on watch at the time and had only taken one bearing, giving a very inaccurate position (you need at least two lines to get a reasonable fix). Denis was reprimanded at the court martial but got away with it.

My stepfather, Charles Ridgway, married Deirdre Murchie, in 1949 and my brother and I had our names legally changed to Ridgway in 1956. Charles (I never addressed him as dad) also served in the Royal Navy in WWII and saw action in the Pacific Theatre aboard the Royal Navy cruiser *HMS Euryalus* as navigation officer. He witnessed a couple of kamikaze attacks on nearby American warships but he never really spoke in detail about it to me. In later years, I wished that both dads had recorded something of their war experiences but most of that generation chose to keep it to themselves.

HMS Euryalus
Stepdad, Sub Lt Charles Ridgway, was navigation officer

A couple of submarine stories I teased out of Denis were his recollections of sailing home to England after a patrol. If a sub was at periscope depth, Coastal Command would attempt to bomb it – whether it was Royal Navy or a German U-Boat. He explained their reasoning was that, to pilots, they all looked the same from the air just below the surface. He reckoned that was the most dangerous part of any patrol and he always tried to return surfaced so he could fly the white RN ensign.

Another story I loved concerned an incident when his sub surfaced in the North Atlantic and not too far away, a U-Boat surfaced at the same time! Both skippers had the shock of their lives and crashed dived immediately.

"We fired off our torpedoes but missed completely!" he said. At that time, subs were pretty primitive and you could not be certain of what was in front of you underwater. His most famous exploit with the chariots off Italy, as mentioned, was not described in any detail – I think that was because it was almost a suicide mission for the frogmen involved. It was incredibly dangerous for Denis too as he had to take his submarine into very shallow water to give the chariots their best chance of success.

*****

After he met my mum, Charles had to leave the navy (it was not done to marry a higher ranking officer's ex-wife in those days) and ended up in the Royal Air Force. Charles had been a sub-lieutenant in the Royal Navy, and Denis a lieutenant commander.

Uncle Alan was in the Army during the war and later in the RAF and retired as a Wing Commander. He had a wonderful sense of humour and there were always plenty of laughs when he was around. Deirdre's brother, Uncle Bill, was in the famous Black Watch regiment that participated in the D-Day landings on the beaches of Normandy in 1944. He was always very anti-American and when drunk would angrily recall how the Yanks had difficulty securing their beachheads even with the help of the Black Watch. His war experiences left him with permanent emotional scars and he never settled back into civilian life after he was de-mobbed as a sergeant. He had a chequered career as a fisherman after the war, among many other jobs. The last I heard of him was from my Aunty Jacko who said that Bill was a hopeless alcoholic living in a caravan somewhere. The Brits were never terribly good at looking after their returned soldiers.

Aunty Jacko was lovely – a very attractive lady with a sunny nature and I loved the holidays I spent with her and Alan and cousin Neil. She was your perfect Aunty, very broadminded and I could talk to her about things I dare not mention at home. At that time, Alan owned a garage in Maldon, Essex and I could earn a little bit of pocket money filling cars with petrol.

Alan bought this old North Sea fishing smack and he and Charles did it up. I even helped to canvas the deck to make it waterproof. It was gaff-rigged, very slow and cumbersome and had a centreboard for stability. A horrible block and tackle arrangement was involved in raising and lowering it. We sailed up the River Crouch out into the North Sea once and I had the job of counting off the numbers on the navigation buoys. The mouth of the Crouch is riddled with sandbars and we did run aground a couple of times, then it was all hands to get that centreboard up so we could get off!

Granny Biddy was lovely too and used to spoil us boys. She laughed a lot and was very tolerant of any naughtiness from her grandsons. Her second husband, John, had been a navy diver during the war. He represented the RN as a boxer so was pretty fit and muscular.

We were a pretty close-knit family and you'll notice that we all called each other by our Christian names. Quite unusual, I suppose, but when you've grown up with it, it sounds ok.

My brother, Mike, had an uneasy career in the RAF before he left and joined the Army. He retired as a Sergeant-Major and still lives in a Yorkshire village called Nafferton. I only hear from him now and then as he's pretty taciturn – he's a real Yorkshireman. We did play together as little kids but after he went off to boarding school it was never the same. One funny story I remember was when I was about eight, I swallowed the brass knob of the opener on my bedroom window. I sat there crying and saying miserably, "I'm going to die, I'm going to die."

"Well, hurry up and get on with it!" Mike replied. A most unsympathetic brother!

I was the black sheep and never joined the services. I wonder how my life would have turned out had I joined the Royal Navy, which was the service I would have chosen. I always dreamed of becoming a fleet-air-arm pilot but my maths were never good enough. I did go on a three day course for pilot aptitude testing at RAF Biggin Hill and really enjoyed the challenge but it was my maths skills that let me down and I failed. I passed the physical component, some of which involved keeping a moving dot inside a circle on a screen with just a joystick and rudder bar for your feet. Maybe the drumming helped my hand-eye co-ordination? I didn't want to join up unless it was as an officer.

Just before I went on that course, Deirdre took me aside and told me that Charles was not my real father. I was sixteen and it was quite a shock. I loved Charles as my dad and still do. He was a really nice man. Denis became more of a friend.

So travel was an integral part of service life. My earliest recollection of overseas travelling was going to Germany where the Brits and the Americans had bases as part of the occupation forces in the 1950s, after the war. We were posted to Sylt in 1957, a small island off the coast of Schleswig-Holstein and right on the border with Denmark. The only way to get there was via a causeway on a train; cars being secured on flat cars behind the passenger carriages. Life on Sylt was great fun in the holidays, especially in summer, as the Germans would flock to the island for nude sunbathing! They made craters in the sand to protect themselves from the wind and just lay about without a stitch of clothing on – we would watch from the nearby sand dunes – lots of laughter for us boys. I recall at a family picnic in the sand dunes one German bloke walked right through our camp completely starkers! Uncle Alan, Charles, Deirdre, Aunty Jacko, my granny Biddy, my brother and I were in stitches for hours after that.

Granny Biddy, John, Mike, me and Whisky, our Alsatian, in the Sylt sand dunes

It was WWII again with the German kids. There were many war orphans on the island and they would wander along the beaches near Westerland, the main town, where we would lie in wait in the sand dunes with our air guns. We would shoot them up the arse with pellets and then run like hell! If we were caught on our own cycling somewhere, the Jerry kids would often get their own back by dragging us off our bikes and giving us a bit of a thumping. Pride was then restored to both sides.

Once, when we were exploring the sand dunes, we came across this metallic thing buried in the sand. I started banging it with my air gun. Then we dug around it. It was an unexploded WWII British bomb! Shit – what irony if it had exploded and killed us British kids. I ran home and told Charles and he arranged for the bomb disposal squad to come out and blow it up. It left a big crater. Was that the second most stupid thing I did? I think it probably was.

Unexploded British WW11 Bomb

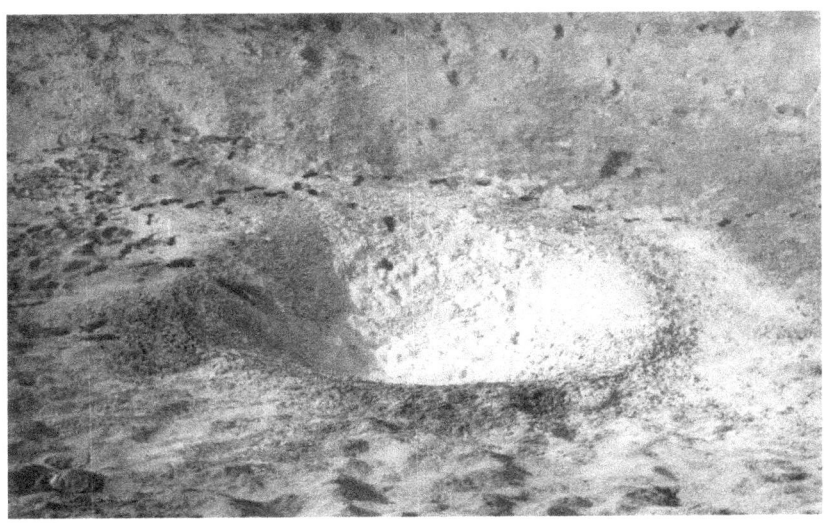

The crater after it was exploded

Another horrible activity, looking back, involved 'stink bombs.' These were little phials of hydrogen sulphide.

Remember high school science classes when you made the stuff and it stank like the most putrid of farts? Well, we could buy these in a novelty shop in Westerland for a few pfennigs (small coins before the Euro) and then we'd seek out a deli, wait for some customers to enter then chuck one in! The ultra-clean German delicatessen would empty in no time and we awful boys would run off laughing.

School was interesting. Children of service parents were sent off to boarding schools scattered around Germany. My brother and I were sent to King Alfred School in Plon, not far from Kiel in Schleswig Holstein. This school was co-ed high with a large enrolment and was divided into five houses – our house was Temple. To get there, we had to take the train from Sylt and then a bus. The school was built around a lake that had been used by the Germans for submarine training before and during the war. It was a large campus, spread over many acres. We kids used the lake for swimming and sailing in summer and in the winter, when it froze over, we used it for tobogganing and skating. We kids were kept busy. In summer, we had lessons in the morning and afternoon and sports in the evening – it stays light until almost 10 pm. In the winter, we had lessons in the morning, sport in the afternoon and then back for more lessons after dinner. Because we shared with girls, there was always a bit of hanky-panky going on which the teachers were mostly oblivious to.

One novel idea was that, in summer, you could skip the morning group shower, which was always in front of our German matron, and have a swim in the lake instead. To obtain this privilege, you had to earn three red strips on your bathers – a feat about the equivalent of getting your lifesaving bronze certificate in Western Australia.

I 'walked out' with a gorgeous blonde girl called Jenny Taplin when I was 14. Holding her hand and kissing her was the stuff of dreams and I would let her walk up the steps into the dining room just ahead of me so I could peek up her skirt at her lovely legs!

Masturbation was rife amongst us boys – we were, after all, testosterone-riddled teenagers. The housemaster, 'Taffy' (a Welshman) was always giving us lectures about excessive 'playing with yourself' and used to say that it would send us blind. The boys ignored him and just sniggered behind his back. We called an orgasm a 'sent' – short for sensations, which were naughty, but nice.

We ate our meals in a large dining room, the long tables set out 'Harry Potter' style with a teacher at the head of each table. We had to mind our table manners and were encouraged to make 'small talk'. The head boy or girl would take turns to say grace before we were allowed to sit down. The prayer was always:

"For what we are about to receive, may the Lord make us truly thankful".

Once, at breakfast the day after we'd had an awful evening meal, the head boy began,

"For what we are about to receive, may the Lord have mercy upon us!"

We all cracked up – but he was caned in front of us, and then expelled. Life was tough.

Friday afternoons were amusing. The sports master would gather all the junior school boys together and announce, "Who likes riding bikes?" Of course, lots of hands went up and he chose about twenty boys. There was no bike riding, though. The boys were taken to the huge oval where the sixth formers (year 12s), who were ATC (Air Training Corps) cadets, were getting a glider ready to fly. The thing was a bit like a flimsy Wright Brothers plane – just a frame fuselage, with canvas wings, a tail plane and fin. The pilot sat in the frame on a seat, strapped in, with the joystick between his legs and a rudder-bar for his feet. The twenty or so lower school boys had to stretch out thick rubber ropes - about 15 boys on each side – as far and taut as they could, like an enormous catapult. The sports teacher would then release the skid under the plane and it would rush off into the air and glide for about a hundred metres. It was huge fun for the pilot. There is no way today, with the current occupational health and safety measures and duty of care, that a 21st century teacher would be allowed to do that activity. I was only caught once for the catapult but boys were conned every week.

I ended up joining the army cadets on Fridays and we would practice marching, playing with .303 rifles and doing all sorts of silly, fun stuff. Summer camp at a real army base was exciting as we even got to ride on a tank. The instructors would also put us through an obstacle course, crawling under nets, climbing up walls, sloshing through mud – all the while firing off thunderflashes in our direction that made deafening bangs! We actually got to fire live ammunition at targets too and we all had to learn to strip down and clean our .303s.

The school had a whole range of sporting options to choose from. One I chose was boxing – what a laugh that was! I was never physically aggressive and the teacher/referee kept encouraging me to hit out. I had three fights, or bouts, all with my best mate, Mick Brown, the school's number one boxer in his age group. We'd just sort of tap each other until the ref stopped the fight and ordered us to get serious – then Mick would give me a couple of hard punches and it was all over. He always said,

"Sorry Nige – I had to do it!

"Yeah, but not for every fight!" I muttered.

Brother Mike was a really good runner. We were known as 'Ridgway 1' and 'Ridgway 2.' Well, Ridgway 2 *was not a runner* and

I hated it. I'd be picked for events like the 220, 440 and 880 yards and come last. An amusing recollection was the Cross Country races, which I really hated. Once, as were nearing the finish, I nicked a bike and cycled for a bit, putting me somewhere in the middle instead of last. I made up for my hatred of running with swimming where I could win races. In fact, to avoid running, I played goalie in soccer, wicket-keeper in cricket and then learnt to sail so I could sit on my arse! Mike won all his running events and even went on to run for the R.A.F.

My love of sailing came from schooldays at KAS and I'll explain all that in a later chapter on sailing and our voyages.

The school was good academically too, with great teachers. I always enjoyed languages and history and we learnt French, German and Latin. By the time we left Germany, I could speak German fairly fluently and understand the written form reasonably well too. Same with French, though I can remember more French than German now. I did win a prize – Homer's *Illiad* –for an essay as I always enjoyed writing too.

Were we ever caned, you ask? Well, yes – and it did hurt. My first time was when I was caught saying the 'f' word on the way into the dining room. Taffy dressed me down in front of the other boys in the common room then I had to wait outside his office upstairs. I poked an exercise book down my pants but, as I bent over, he saw the bulge and pulled it out. He said,

"This is going to hurt me more than it is you!"

Stupid comment! I think I got four good ones across the arse and it was hard to sit down for a couple of days after. I had red welts too but I didn't cry. If we were caught talking after lights out, the duty teacher would come barging into the dorm and the culprit (sometimes me) would have to bend over the end of his bed and get a couple of good slaps on his arse with a slipper.

There was a sort of honour system amongst us boys. If caught out and the teacher couldn't identify the culprit immediately, we would all own up. One boy would be picked and take the punishment – I suppose a bit like in the movie, *"Spartacus"* where Kirk Douglas stands and says he's Sparticus, then, one by one, all his mates stand and declare that they are Spartacus too.

One of the great things we were allowed to do at school was to roller skate down to the dining room, which was a fair distance from Temple House. As we were so busy, I don't ever recall being homesick, bored or bullied.

My wife, Aileen, and I visited the old school in 2015 as guests of the Germans, who have taken back the campus as a NATO training academy. You can imagine Aileen's delight to be met at the gates by two handsome German Officers who were our guides for the day!

*****

That wasn't my first boarding school. The first was when I was just a little tacker of eight. It was called Cokethorpe and was situated in Aylesbury, Buckinghamshire. I still have awful memories of walking down a platform at Paddington Station in London, past the big wheels and the hissing and streaming of the engine. Then Charles would put my case onto the overhead rack and I'd spend the whole journey to Aylesbury paranoid that I wouldn't be able to get it down. My parents had no idea about all this and I never told them until years later as an adult – they were horrified, after all I was only a little boy. How does that affect you as an adult? I think it had quite an impact on me and has made me a bit weary of getting too close to people for fear of abandonment or being rejected. And I also think that the bouts of depression may have come from those years. The 'black dog,' as Churchill described it, has visited me on quite a few occasions in my life. It leaves you feeling utterly helpless and it's no use anyone saying, "Come on. Get over it," because life, at that time, has no meaning, and helpful platitudes like that really are meaningless. You don't feel sad – *you feel nothing*. If you are lucky enough not to suffer, then you'll never know what it's like – those that have suffered will know *exactly* what I mean. I have learnt to live with it and realise that the cloud will pass and the sun will shine again.

Sometimes matron would tuck us in at night and give us a little pat on the head and that human contact was precious. We had to do jobs ('fag') – for the older boys, things like polishing their shoes or carrying books and sporting gear. If you refused or jacked up, the big boys would give you a good thumping. It didn't happen to me but I'm sure bullying was rife. Boys with wealthier parents would receive parcels of 'tuck', which contained sweets (lollies), cake and biscuits. Weak boys could use the tuck for protection from the bullies but, of course, there was no way out once you did that. No one would tell teachers or parents. Memories of that school experience are a bit vague so I guess it wasn't enjoyable, unlike KAS.

*****

After Germany, we returned to England and a posting to Suffolk. There was an RAF radar station at Bawdsey, right on the North Sea and the married quarters were three miles away in the village of Alderton. I completed year 10 and 11 at St Peter's School in Felixstowe. The trip to school involved a three-mile cycle to Bawdsey to get the ferry across the River Deben in all weathers, then a bus or cycle ride of three more miles to school. The skipper of the ferry was an ex-fisherman and it was incredible how he could motor the vessel crab-wise against the strong tidal flows and then head up at the last minute to tie up to the jetty without a bump.

The school was pretty easy going after Germany and I didn't put much into my studies. Rock 'n' Roll was beginning to make its presence felt more and more. I became really good friends with our local Rector's sons in Alderton, Barry and Garth, and we got up to lots of mischief in the village. They both went to St Peter's too. Garth loved language, like me, and we would often have punning sessions. Two I remember and love were about two of the boys: We had a kid named Paddy Riches – I used to say:

"A good name is better than riches!"

Garth would counter with one for a kid named Murphy, who had an older, bigger, brother – you guessed it: "Thank heaven for small murphy's!" (Mercies).

Garth became an English high school teacher and later got into buying and selling weapons and armoury, becoming quite wealthy. Sadly he died in a traffic accident when his car aquaplaned and left the road, hitting a tree. He was only 63. We keep in contact with Barry and see him on UK visits. He married a village girl, Ginny, and still lives in Alderton, having bought the Rectory from the Church of England. They call their home 'Rectory House'. He's made lots of money from life insurance.

One poor teacher at St Peter's was called Mr Unthank – he had coke-bottle glasses, a reedy voice, baggy trousers that were too short and wild hair. We gave him heaps! Once, Paddy Riches rigged up a length of thin copper wire from his desk to a light over Unthank's desk. He attached a paper plane to it and, by pulling it unseen, could get the wings to flap. Of course we all cracked up but poor old Unthank never worked it out. The headmaster, Mr Robinson, who taught us maths and science, saw the funny side but did not see the funny side when I wrote in the condensation on the window near me,

"Robbo is a bum!" That got me a whack.

The best teacher at the school was Rector Vincent. He taught us English, English literature and R.I. (religious instruction). R.I. was always a part of our curriculum at all the schools I attended and I did find the stories very interesting but was never a believer.

Back at the village, a bloke used to buy black market cigarettes from the Americans (there was a USAF base a few miles up the road) and flog them off to the villagers, us included, for a small profit. We used to break into his shed and nick packets of ciggies knowing full well that he couldn't tell the local bobby, as he'd be in trouble too. Barry looked a bit older than the rest of us and he would get pints of beer from the local pub that we'd drink out the back. My parents would have been horrified!

Occasionally the local policeman would chase us on his bike but he never managed to catch us. If he spoke to our parents, we would always put on our best manners and my mum and the Rector's wife would dismiss his complaints – "It's just horseplay – boys will be boys!"

Teenage boys are awful. Once, the fattest girl in the village – who was madly in love with Barry – stripped naked for him and we stole her clothes; the three of us rolling around laughing while she walked home naked through the woods. We gave her clothes back just before she got home and she, amazingly, saw the funny side herself.

Another funny incident happened when one of the other officer's daughters, Gillian, invited a school friend to stay with her. Her dad put up a tent in the back garden for them. (The married quarters were very close to each other). Well, Barry and I chatted up the girls and arranged to see them late at night in the tent. The plan was for me to attach a piece of string to my toe, throw the end out of my bedroom window – and Barry would give it a tug to wake me at midnight. Of course, I was so excited that I couldn't sleep anyway so I tied the string to my bed leg. When Barry started tugging on it – I leant out and poured a cup of water over him!

We crept into the tent for a bit of heavy petting, me with Gillian. After about an hour, I went home to bed but Barry stayed a while longer – lots of laughter and giggling going on. This woke up Gillian's dad and he approached the tent with a cricket bat, shouting, "Get out, Ridgway!"

Barry emerged from the tent and said he'd just come to collect a book – the irate dad chased him down the road with the bat! Did we all laugh about that the next day – even our parents saw the funny side! The Rector was highly amused too and his dear wife just shook her head.

*****

I fell in love with 'Cuckoo', a gorgeous well-developed 15 year old who was very flirtatious and promiscuous. She fell for me too and one afternoon took me home to her place in Felixstowe after school while her mum was at work.

"Do you want me to peel?" she said.

"What, spuds?" I naively replied.

She said nothing and began to take off all her clothes and led me to her bed.

It was heaven! I got home late that day but my mum just wanted to know if I'd had fun.

"Yeah," I mumbled, as teenage boys do.

Due to all this activity, schoolwork lagged behind and I only passed three 'O' levels in the GCE exams – English, English Lit. and French.

The summer after the exams I spent with another lovely girl, Vicki. Her family had one of those beach huts on the pebbly Felixstowe beach and we used it to explore each other's bodies for hours on end there. We were both in love at 16 and schoolwork was the last thing on our minds. Vicki was really lovely – she had a neat figure, long dark hair and brown eyes. She had a great sense of humour and we laughed a lot at the silliest things. It was a wonderful summer. Vicki was also musical and played the violin, having proper classical music tuition. Of course, as a budding rock 'n' roll drummer, I teased her unmercifully. I wonder where she is now? She probably became a professional classical musician.

Chapter Three

Off to the Middle East – Jordan

Jordan seeks to play only one role, that of a model state. It is our aim to set an example for our Arab brethren ..."

King Hussein

Another posting interrupted that summer reverie. Charles announced that he'd been posted to Jordan to work with the Jordanian Air Force. Deirdre, ever the more adventurous of the two, suggested that we drive there, which we did. There was a huge amount of planning involved and the British AA Club helped with maps and directions. Charles involved me in the planning, as I'd always loved maps and things.

Charles bought a new little Morris Minor Shooting Brake (station wagon in Oz) and we all piled in with our cases and our large German shepherd dog, Whisky. Brother Michael was in the air force by now. It was a crazy trip but what an adventure. We drove through Holland, Germany, Austria, Greece, Yugoslavia, Turkey, Syria and finally into Jordan. That was in 1962 and I can't remember how long it took, but it was some weeks. Some of the backroads were atrocious in Yugoslavia, Turkey and Syria and I had to get out of the car in places to move large stones so we could get through. My mum took Whisky into every hotel with us and into every restaurant and café we ate at. She just walked out if they refused to allow our dog in. I had always been a 'meat and two veg' sort of kid but my tastes were extended on that trip because we ate what the locals ate wherever we went. Some of the 'hotels' were literally fleapits and bed bugs bit us on many occasions.

Driving through Belgrade, Yugoslavia, I wound down the window and exclaimed, much to Charles's horror, "Look at all those communists!"

Driving through Syria was interesting. Bedouin hospitality meant that if you stopped at a village for petrol or a bite to eat, you'd have to have a faltering chat and cup of hot, sweet tea or really strong Turkish coffee. Turkish coffee has grouts in the bottom of the little cups and the first time I tasted it, I swallowed some – ugh!

Exploring Crusader castles was a highlight. There are about eleven of these scattered around that part of the Middle East and they were bastions of Christian defence during the Crusades before Saladin drove the Crusaders out. Charles was a great history buff and could fill us in on the details. Looking back now, it was probably quite dangerous driving though Syria. The country had only just become independent in 1961. Before that, it had an uneasy alliance with Egypt from 1958 as the United Arab Republic with a view to destroying the newly formed state of Israel (1948). There were many coups in the 60s until the Ba'ath Party and Assad family took over. Of course, I had no knowledge of this in 1962 as I was only 16.

Jordan itself was a really interesting place. I completed my secondary education there in a joint Jordanian/ex-pat school. Most of the Jordanian Arabs we mixed with were refugees from Palestine and the tension between them and the Israelis was quite evident to us – although I knew little about the politics at that time. Soldiers from both sides carried guns and walked the streets of Jerusalem quite casually as the ancient city was divided in two halves in the 60s, before the Seven Day War of 1967. We were given a house on Jebel Amman (jebel means hill in Arabic) in Amman. It had lovely views of the city and was quite spacious.

I made friends with other ex-pat guys my age but there were no girls. We visited Palestinian Christian girls at their homes but they were always so well chaperoned that all we could do was fantasise about them. We could not quite get used to Arab boys walking around holding hands – they were probably only friends but we wanted to hold the hands of girls.

Our group was made up from kids from the UK, US, Austria and Yugoslavia. My best friends were brothers: Peter and Dodi, who both ended up emigrating to Australia as well so we do keep in touch. They both had careers as flight attendants for Qantas; Dodi lives in Sydney and Peter lives in Perth. Like many brothers, including mine, they don't keep in touch with each other.

After school in Amman, we would wander down to the Philadelphia Hotel swimming pool and muck about there, hoping to chat up the floor-show dancers. As ex-pats we were well received by the Arabs, except during Ramadan. Then we'd have to be careful walking around as we'd get stones chucked at us. I had my own driver to take me to school and we had a cook/housekeeper at home to do most of the work for my mum so I suppose we were almost treated like minor royalty.

Weekends were spent exploring and we visited all the Biblical sights and towns, having 'swims' in the Dead Sea and drives down to Aqaba where the snorkelling among the reefs was fantastic. King Hussein had a holiday home at Aqaba that he allowed us ex-pats to use. I got horribly sunburnt one weekend and was in agony for the long drive back to Amman. Our cook told me to spread yoghurt over the redness and it worked a treat, taking the pain and heat away immediately. It was a remedy I've always remembered.

The best part of the drive to Aqaba was going past Wadi Rum where they filmed the desert scenes for *Lawrence of Arabia*, which they finished in 1961, just before we got to Jordan. We would stop at Bedouin tents and they would offer us hot, black, sweet tea that was surprisingly refreshing. The scenery was like a combination of moonscape and Mars, reddish with some grey.

Petra was another amazing experience. Donkey rides through the narrow chasm brought us to the extraordinary façade of the old city. We took granny Biddy there once and the locals let her ride a donkey in through the narrow gap. She was thrilled. Deirdre was a blonde then and villagers would follow us through the streets, little kids wanting to touch her hair.

Biddy enters Petra on a donkey.

Very narrow gap into ancient Petra

All this exploring was done before mass tourism that began with cheaper air travel in the mid-sixties, this causing the demise of the cruise ships of that time. We, and the other ex-pats, were the only Westerners we met up with in Jordan. In Bethlehem and Jerusalem there were small numbers of tourists but not the huge crowds of today. Calvary, where Jesus was supposed to have been crucified, was very moving – as was the Garden of Gethsemane, locals claiming that some of the olive trees were 2,000 or more years old. In Bethlehem, we visited the Church of Nativity, which is the sacred site believed to be Christ's birthplace. With fewer tourists then, in later life my mother used to say that the 'common man' has spoilt travel. Sitting in an airport these days, I think she had a point.

One other historical site worth mentioning was the ancient Roman city of Jerash, about 30 miles north of Amman. Some of the most perfectly preserved Roman ruins in the Middle East are here – long streets with grooves cut in them from years of chariots being driven through the city; intact temples and homes can be seen and you feel steeped in history. Jerash has an almost perfect amphitheatre and it was not hard to imagine plays and music being performed there. The acoustics are so good – even after nearly 2,000 years.

Poor Whisky was sixteen years old by now and was becoming very frail. Deirdre and Charles just could not bear the thought of having him put down. One morning he began to whimper and I sat on the floor with him. He put his head on my lap and just peacefully passed away into doggy heaven. It was a beautiful moment that I wished Deirdre could have experienced but she just could not face it. Charles buried him at the end of the runway at Amman airport.

We all loved Jordan and the privileged life we led. Doors were open to us as the king was kindly disposed towards British officers, himself being a graduate of Sandhurst. He gave Charles a lovely gold watch with the Jordanian Crown engraved on it that I have inherited. Charles made friends with other Jordanian officers, and the radar station he helped establish near Amman pleased the king. Unfortunately, it was one of the first things the Israelis attacked during the 1967 Seven Day War and many of those friends were killed. I suppose we always thought the Palestinians had a good argument for a separate state and – after all these years of war and terrorism – I still firmly believe that to be the case.

King Hussein is dead now and his first born son (to an English girl), Abdullah II, is king. Jordan has a sort of democracy and probably is the most stable of the Arab countries in the region, having an uneasy peace with Israel.

For a really good insight into the Arab/Israeli conflict (and hatreds) have a read of Colum McCann's excellent book, 'Apeirogon.' (2020). In it, he explores the relationship between a Jew, Rami, and a Palestinian Arab, Bassam. Rami's daughter was killed by an Arab suicide bomber and Bassam's daughter was shot and killed by an Israeli border patrol soldier. Together, the two men have managed to see this awful conflict from the other's point of view, and developed a strong friendship. They tour the world and the Middle East promoting peace and dialogue between the two sides. Let's hope the movement grows.

I was about seventeen and a half when I received a letter from Guy, a friend in England, asking me to join a band they were forming to play around London. I had finished school with three GCE 'O' levels (I never passed any 'A' levels) and was ready to leave home, so I wrote back to say that I'd join the band. My parents were very sceptical, so I had to have a second string to my bow which was a letter of introduction to a telegraph company in Dagenham, East London, where they hoped I might get an apprenticeship in laying telephone cables and so on, to become a technician.

The flight back to England was slow but interesting as we flew in a four-engined propeller plane, a Britannia, and passed right over the Alps. I could see the mountaintops quite clearly not far below from my window seat.

I took a taxi all the way from Stansted Airport out to my friend's place in Stanmore, North London, much to his amusement.

Thus began a new chapter in my life as a drummer in an R&B (rhythm & blues) band in London.

Chapter Four

Musical Awakenings

"Musicians don't retire; they stop when there's no more music in them."   Louis Armstrong

My first recollection of an awakening interest in music and drums was Louis Armstrong's All-Stars band on an EP (extended play vinyl record) recorded in Germany (1953). That was in 1958 and I must have been thirteen. The track was *"Tiger Rag"* with a fantastically fast drumming intro from Barrett Deems – then, later on in the number, Louis lets Barrett go berserk again on the kit. The crowd are yelling for more and off he goes again. I used to listen to that track over and over again and I still love it.

The next drummer to catch my attention was Sandy Nelson, who had a couple of solo hits in the 60s – *Teen Beat* and *Let There Be Drums*. Guitar riffs punctuated the solos and I loved the rhythms, which were not as frantic as *Tiger Rag* but very appealing to me.

I also listened to a bit of Gene Krupa and Louis Bellson but I didn't like the big band sound back then. Another incredibly fast drummer was Buddy Rich who could play amazing solos just using his snare drum. I'm still amazed at his work when I check it out on You Tube.

I loved the drummers with Elvis, Buddy Holly, Chuck Berry and lots of other pop artists. I became a fan of Tony Meehan from The Shadows (Cliff Richards's backing band). He had a neat, clean technique. Their early records are so well produced and Tony is featured on most of them. When he left The Shadows, he was replaced by Brian Bennett, another fine drummer who is still playing today. I last saw him at Burswood Entertainment Centre when The Shadows and Cliff Richard got together for a 50th anniversary tour. He was superb!

The first band we got together was a skiffle group. This was simple guitar stuff with a tea-chest bass and me playing drums on boxes after I had been demoted as the tea-chest bass player. That was at high school in Germany (KAS).

The first real band was formed in our village in Suffolk. We had lead guitar, rhythm guitar, bass guitar and drums – the same line-up as The Shadows and countless other bands at the time. We practised out in our garage, or down at the Rectory. School friend Barry still has one of our original homemade amplifiers in his garage – it was made up from pirated bits and valves of old radios. The band name, *'Bee Vincent and The Voodoos'* is still on the front! I remember waiting for my first snare drum to arrive in the village. I had ordered it by mail and waited everyday for the parcel to arrive in the delivery truck. When it did – wow! But what to do with it? I learnt to play the beat for "Riders in the Sky" – that was our very first tune. I added a bass drum and small-tom, both second-hand from Sandy Sutherland, a year 12 student at school who had a band as well. For the floor tom, I moulded some particle board around a steaming kettle for hours, added a rim and skin and some wooden legs and there it was. I had to make my own bass drum pedal too. A cheap cymbal completed the 'kit' and I was off and running. The second instrumental we learnt was 'Apache' by The Shadows (every garage band learnt that one).

The Voodoos, 1960. Barry (Bee) Vincent took the photo!

The band was pretty amateurish, but we had lots of fun. We once hired the local hall and put on a dance. We decorated the place, did all the posters and took the door take, which wasn't much, but we did have a tidy little crowd.

Our first paid gig was for a wedding. One of the village girls and an American serviceman from the base up the road got married and we were asked to play. There were many Yanks at that wedding and they micky-finned my Cokes. I ended up absolutely plastered. I knocked my drums over and crawled off the stage crying out, "The Zulus are coming, the Zulus are coming!"

I ended up at the Rectory and the next morning I had my first really painful hangover. My mother came down to the rectory in the morning and she was really angry with me – I'd never her seen her get quite so mad before. "This is not the behaviour of an officer's son, etc, etc!!!" My head hurt too much to care.

We actually became quite a good band by the time I left for Jordan. My drum kit improved with the addition of a hi-hat and proper bass drum pedal. We organised our own dances and played at school socials. When you live in a small English village you learn to make your own fun and playing in the band gave us all heaps of satisfaction. My parents could never really understand it all and, unfortunately, never showed enough interest for me to take formal drum lessons so that I could learn to read music and the correct rudiments (basic drum patterns). I was self-taught.

I packed the drums into a wooden crate and they were shipped out to Jordan with all our other stuff. I didn't play for some months after that. In Jordan, I was able to do an occasional sit-in at the nightclub at the Philadelphia Hotel but there were no other young musicians around to get a band going. I enjoyed the nightclub and got by, even though I couldn't read a dot of the music scores.

It was quite a relief when Guy Price contacted me and said we should get a band going in London.

We called the band *The Temeraires*, after that famous painting by Turner, '*The Fighting Temeraire*'. Guy, being an artist himself, loved that painting. He was also a fine bass player. The line up was lead guitar, rhythm guitar, bass, drums and a vocalist/harmonica player. It was early 1963 and The Beatles were all the rage with their hit, *Love me Do*. We liked The Rolling Stones and rhythm and blues bands more. There was a huge R&B scene in London in the early sixties, quite different to the pop culture in the rest of Britain and the 'Mersey Sound' from up north, especially Liverpool. We got gigs as first band on with bands like The Yardbirds, The Stones, Georgie Flame and the Blue Flames, Chris Farlowe and The Thunderbirds, John Myall's Blues Breakers, Long John Baldry and other bands similar to ourselves. We played at The Flamingo Club, The Craw Daddy Club in Richmond, Finsbury Park and Eel Pie Island in the middle of the River Thames. We also did gigs in pubs and other clubs that featured blues bands. It was a fantastic time musically as there were so many great players around. It was just as much fun watching other bands as it was playing. The Yardbirds had a unique thing where they doubled up the tempo in a 12-bar blues (from a shuffle to really fast triplets) – what with the lights flashing in unison with it, the crowd went nuts, almost in a trance! Eric Clapton was playing lead with them at the time and he was incredible, even in his late teens. I loved Georgie Fame's band. He sounded so cool and he had a big black bloke playing a conga drum, making the band look and sound exotic.

The Temeraires - I'm at the back

My two favourite drummers to go and watch were Red Reece with Georgie Fame and Phil Seaman, who played modern jazz. It was cheap, or free, to go to pubs and clubs. One night, when we were booked to go on before Georgie Fame, Red let me use his kit and gave me a bit of advice about 'driving' a band. I never forgot it.

Those clubs were thick with smoke – it almost hurt to breathe and I probably got the bout of bladder cancer I had later in life from all the passive smoking. We didn't care then as we all smoked and the music scene was so incredibly interesting. It's difficult to appreciate just how exciting that era of blues in London was.

A memorable gig was on Eel Pie Island in the Thames. It was mid-winter, bloody cold, and we had to carry the gear over the footbridge to get to the hall. It was very slippery underfoot. Once inside it was really warm, and thick with smoke and the scent of marijuana. Lots of couples were lying about, some shagging going on and a heavy air of decadence. Red let me use part of his kit again as we were first on. The crowd went nuts when we played a Bo Diddly song with that pounding tom-tom beat! We got £5 for the gig. Not long ago, I Googled some of the records of the gigs at Eel Pie on the internet and found *'Temeraires'* - £5 and *'Rolling Stones'* £35.

Our band earnt an average of about £5 a night – £1 for our roadie and the rest split between us. We had to get day jobs to support ourselves and I worked in various factories around London as a storeman. I remember one job I had with Dixon Photographics. They wanted me to train to be a camera technician and repairman (I was 18 at the time) but I had no patience for the fiddly bits and was always thinking about the band and the next gig. Some Japanese guys were employed by Dixon's to fix cameras and to help train us Poms and I had quite a laugh with the language difficulties. They were so serious and dedicated to their work, almost like robots.

Sadly, *The Temeraires* eventually broke up as the lead guitarist, Dave Basham, moved out of London and Guy wanted to concentrate on his painting. Guy became quite well known in London and ended up doing restorations of old masters at the National and Tate Galleries. Regrettably, he died at 49 after years as a diabetic – he was never a good patient. Dave Basham stills plays in the pubs of Norfolk. I don't know what happened to the harmonica player, Roscoe, or the rhythm guitarist, Malcolm. For a while we were very busy around London and I thought we'd make it, as you do when young and enthusiastic.

I went back home for a while after the band broke up. My folks were posted back to Suffolk from Jordan and I went to live with them again for a short time. I would make trips up to London to see Guy and we would go out together to check out bands. I bought an ancient car, a left-hand drive Opel, and Guy and I decided to do a painting and writing trip to Cornwall. The trip ended in disaster.

The Opel was my first car, a clapped out cheapie that only cost me ten quid. The main bearings were stuffed and it blew black smoke constantly. Charles gave me a hand to replace the bearings – just a stopgap measure as they wouldn't last without the crankshaft being machined. Anyway, I drove up to London and picked up Guy. We headed off to Cornwall, the plan being that Guy would do some charcoal portraits of punters that he hoped to sell and I'd write some poetry (I was into poetry then, my favourite poets being William Blake and T.S Eliot). Well we did sell a few portraits but it was not a roaring success. On the way back home, we were driving through Somerset, not far from my birthplace, along narrow country lanes when disaster struck. It was late at night and I was getting tired so I asked Guy to take over the driving. I climbed into the back seat with my legs over the front seat and fell asleep. Next thing I knew, there was a huge *Bang!* We must have hit a tree or something, I thought, as I groggily woke up. I crawled out the left hand back door and sat on the grass verge. The car was steaming and looked a wreck.

"Fuck, Guy, what's happened?"

"We hit a lorry. It only had one inside light and I thought it was a motorbike!".

"Shit, I can't move my legs. I'd better stay here. Bloody hell, it's only insured for me so I'll have to say I was driving."

Then I lost consciousness. I woke up in an ambulance and my knees were in agony, every bump in the road adding to the pain. Next morning I found myself in hospital in Taunton, my legs in plaster from the ankles to the hips. The surgeon said I was lucky to be alive. He also said I would have arthritic problems in later life. He was not wrong – I had a right knee replacement in 2005 and the left leg is following the right leg! Guy had a big gash on his forehead but was otherwise ok but in shock.

"The lorry had a load of apples on board; they were scattered all over the road," explained Guy. Later we learnt that the local villagers nicked them all. The farmer sued us for damages and loss of his produce but a London QC was sent down to Somerset to be my counsel (by my insurance company) and we won the case. I had to perjure myself and keep repeating to the judge that the lorry only had one inside light and looked like a motorbike. I was awarded some damages and spent $800 of it on an MG TF in Australia. Another silly decision, as I should have put a deposit on a small house.

MG TF – My first car in WA

*****

The next band was in Australia. I eventually ended up in Perth, and was looking for a way to get back into music. I walked into Clef Music shop in Hay street in '68 to enquire about a set of drums and met Rod Christian, who sold me a Droun kit. I also bumped into Ron Burns who was forming a band called *The Blue Brass*. I auditioned and got the gig and worked in that band until around 1970.

The Blue Brass was a very versatile band and we covered a

whole range of music. We scored a regular gig at the Nanking Theatre Restaurant in Belmont. The Nanking opened seven nights a week then and we landed the Thursday to Sunday sessions, backing cabaret and floorshow artists, as well as entertaining the diners and dancers ourselves. We had two in-house singers to entertain with us – Kelly Green and Michelle Edwards. Our band had Elaine Mort as a vocalist. The Nanking was amazingly popular and was absolutely packed to the rafters on the weekends. The strippers were always the most awkward to back – they lived under the illusion that they were 'artistes' and got really annoyed if I got the bumps and grinds out of synch. I could never read music well enough to sight-read for the floorshows so I used to bluff my way through. I used to give the boys in the band a laugh by putting the drum music charts on my stand upside-down!

The Nanking was a Chinese restaurant and was very popular in its heyday. What killed it was an article in the *Sunday Times* that proclaimed the cooks were using cats in their recipes. They were not, of course, but the whole incident came from compere Peter Harries who used to tell jokes about cats in the food as part of his act. The rumour went round Perth like wildfire and the restaurant never recovered.

I left that band after an argument with Ron and went on to join another band with Rod Christian and Peter Waterman. Rod had been in *The Blue Brass* band too. The new band was a good old rock 'n' roll band and we did quite well on the Perth pub circuit. We called ourselves *Motivation*. In those days, the Swan Hotel group owned lots of pubs and employed bands from Wednesday through to the Sunday session. Once you were on the circuit (after an audition) a band could look forward to four or five regular gigs a week. I think that's why Perth bands in the 60's and 70's were so good. We all had regular work and there was a lot of competition among the bands. We would do a pub gig until about 10:30 and then go on to play at a nightclub.

I left *Motivation* in less than happy circumstances. I had a minor accident in my car on the way to catch the Rottnest ferry for a gig on the island and missed the ferry. They got another drummer to fill in and he ended up taking my place. Not a very pleasant outcome.

Nearly all the Perth musos used to work day jobs too, as there was just not quite enough money in playing to do it full-time. I reckon all musos give so much of their leisure time to the public – missing out on Christmas, New Year's Eve and other celebrations with families, they're always there playing away while the 'punters' are having fun. I guess our compensation was that our hobby was paying us money and we always had the opportunity to meet girls.

Anyway, I was working at Peerless Emulsion as their warehouse supervisor when I received a call from Port Hedland. It was from Bill Blaine, a country and western guitarist and singer who was looking for a drummer to play seven nights a week at the Esplanade Hotel up there. It didn't take me long to say, "Yes!" as the money was more than double what I was earning in the polish factory. My wife agreed to let me go.

I bundled the drums onto a plane and flew up a few days later. What a shock! It was early December and the heat was stifling and hit me like a sledgehammer. Everything was covered in red dust and it looked a most inhospitable place. The Esplanade was a rambling hotel, pretty dirty, with a large beer garden where the band played every night. The rickety old stage had seen better years and it looked like a lean-to shed out in the bush. The band gear was kept in a locked-up cool room and we had to lug it out each night to set up on stage. The place was packed every night – mainly with single guys working in the mining industry. There were quite a few T-I's (Thursday Islanders) still in town. Those guys had helped with the rail construction. After a few beers, look out as they were always spoiling for a punch-up! I became friends with one of them when I did at bit of labouring at the nearby Shell Depot during the day. His name was Tom-Tom and he helped show me how to handle full 44-gallon drums with ease. He'd make me laugh as he kept saying, "Bless ma heart and bless ma soul – I ain't never seen a nigger with a white asshole!" as he threw around the drums of fuel, laughing away! He was as black as the ace of spades. He'd get roaring drunk at the 'Nard' as we called it, but he never hit me, acting more like a bodyguard.

The band was great. We had a really good lead guitarist, Gabe Zentai and great bass player, John Hunter. Bill handled most of the C&W vocals. It was easy for me to fit in and I really enjoyed the county music, especially the rockabilly stuff that was up-tempo with a fast skippy beat. The crowd loved us and we pulled more people than the rock 'n' roll band over the road at the Pier Hotel.

It was so hot that we had to change shirts at least twice a night or we'd end up drenched with sweat after a couple of songs. We played from eight till eleven and until midnight on the weekends.

That pub held the record for the most kegs of beer drunk in a week – forty of them! The average Perth pub might do three or four, to show the comparison. We earned a bit of extra dough by picking the kegs up from the wharf, rolling then off the refrigerated truck into the pub's cool room. Bill scored a job selling new Chrysler cars and Toyota 4-wheel drives and did really well for a while – mainly because he offered ridiculous prices for his trade-ins. I was asked to set-up a spare parts department, though I'd never had any experience at that. The nor'west was like that, you just had a go. It was hard work, but fun and I could eventually quote some part numbers from memory without having to look them up the parts book. I have to admit that it was frustrating for travellers who came in looking for specific parts – we just could not hold stock for every part – and I would tell them, "The part's available ex-east!" The place ultimately went broke due to Bill's high trade-in deals and the losses incurred when it came time to sell them. It was fun while it lasted.

The Esplanade hotel employed quite a few barmaids and housemaids, all young like us guys in the band. There was bound to be a little bit of mischief going on and it was not really a surprise when I found one of the lovely little housemaids in my bed after we'd finished playing one night! I feel bad about it now but at the time it was very exciting and all I can think of is Oscar Wilde's adage, "I can resist anything except temptation." That was the beginning of a non-stop flow of girls, which of course, had a devastating effect on my marriage. I'll come back to this in a later chapter.

Nothing lasts forever and the band broke up when Bill decided to go back to Perth as he'd saved enough to buy a house.

I was offered another job in a band working at the Hedland Motor Hotel. This was a three-piece effort with squeeze-box (accordion), sax and drums. We played lots of German 'oom-pah' music that was great fun for the drinkers. It was some months before we realised that the Dutch bandleader on the squeezebox was ripping us off. He'd nip into the toilets after the Sunday session with the band payments and then come back out to 'share' the proceeds. One afternoon, we followed him in and caught him red-handed pocketing extra for himself. We didn't say much, but I had a quiet word with the manager and said I could get a much better band for the pub if he sacked the Dutchman. The manager agreed. The guy was sacked and I got Tony Tyler up from Perth to form a new band.

We called this band *Purple Haze* – the name was really a send-up of heavy metal bands. We were far from heavy metal and our repertoire included instrumentals, early rock 'n' roll and some of the latest chart toppers. There were four of us – Tony Tyler on guitar and vocals, Greg (Bazz) on sax/trumpet and vocals, Bill on lead guitar and vocals, and myself. We didn't have a bass player at first as we couldn't find one in Hedland. It didn't matter. The band was really successful and we packed the Hedland Motor Hotel from Wednesday through to Sunday. Tony was very talented and could mimic most artists. His speciality was Elvis and, if you closed your eyes, you would swear it was Elvis. The nor'westers loved him. While we were performing at the Hedland, it became the place to go for entertainment as it was much more comfortable than the Esplanade or Pier, being air-conditioned. It was at this gig I first began to sing a couple of vocals myself, after lots of encouragement from Tony.

We all did some day jobs. I worked as a spare-parts man for Coventry Motors, Bazz worked as a fitter and turner for Hamersley Iron, Tony did some work around the pub and Bill flogged used cars.

One summer while we were there, a cyclone hit the town and the cars parked outside the Hedland Motor Hotel got sandblasted. The hotel was on the beach, overlooking the ocean. It was amazing as one side of the cars still had paint whereas the other side was down to bare metal. I was living in a transportable home alongside the hotel with my family and we had to barricade the front window with beds, wardrobes and mattresses to stop it from blowing in.

Eventually we all had enough of the nor'west and decided to get back to Perth. We lined up a job in Mandurah at the Silver Sands Hotel and made our way there. I towed a 20-foot caravan down and the other guys drove or caught a plane.

The Mandurah gig wasn't a huge success and we all began to yearn for the warmth of the north after a couple of months. Our decision to go was precipitated by one of the local hoons who put toilet paper on our stage! Bazz, our nuggety sax player, gave the guy a thump in the gents and we never had any more trouble, but our minds were made up anyway.

Tony and I did some negotiations with the Walkabout Hotel group and landed a contract to play at Karratha for three months, then at Geraldton. It was good regular money and we were by now fully professional. We added a bass player, Harry, to the line up to improve our sound.

Then began a couple of years of the most fun I think any of us had ever had in a band. The band was enormously popular in Karratha. We began to do floorshows on the weekend and that brought in even more people. We never did the same thing twice as we always got together on Mondays to nut out new ideas and to rehearse. My job was to introduce the floorshow with a joke, and then we all did a turn out the front.

Purple Haze at the Walkabout Hotel, Karratha – Tony out front.

I remember magician acts with Bill, The Indy 500 Car Race raced around the dance floor on my kids tricycles, Bazz doing a Barry Mackenzie impersonation, Harry doing Roy Orbison (The Big 'O') and Tony topping the bill with his Elvis impersonation – complete with the full sequined jump-suit. He could even walk on his hands while singing Elvis, which the crowd roared at!

We had many changes of shirts, pants and a full three-piece suit that we began the evening with. We looked great – and the crowd never knew what we were going to wear as we always mixed and matched the shirts and pants for variety. It was another way of selling the band and providing novelty for the 'punters'.

The Geraldton gig was memorable too. Walkabout offered us a fibro house on the seafront for our accommodation and we immediately set about painting its front facade purple. This caused lots of talk around the town and the DJ at the local radio station often referred to it as the 'Purple Pad' and would announce that there would be a party on that night after we finished playing. There *was* a party on every night after we finished playing and I reckon about half the young people in Geraldton were there – especially the girls. We had no problem with guys coming along too as long as there was no trouble. One night we did have some yobbos who wanted to get in. They were aggressive and threatened us with knives if we wouldn't open the doors. We went out to try and pacify them but they became more agro, so Bazz thumped one of them, knocking him over a low brick wall. That cured them, they left quietly and we never had any more bother.

We had the stereo blaring away, dancing was going on and if we fancied one of the girls, we'd slip away into one of the bedrooms. It was all harmless fun, really. No drugs except booze and anyone was free to stay the night if they were too pissed to drive home. We always kicked them out before breakfast – except the girls in our beds. They would help us guys clean up and prepare brekky. When we wandered into town, we would always stop and chat to the locals and I think that all helped with the band's popularity. Many musicians were pasty faced, unhealthy-looking guys with long, lank hair, but we always kept fit and enjoyed the pool so we were tanned and fresh-looking.

A very fit rock 'n' roll band! Morning P.T!

The three months there were really good fun and we got tighter and tighter as a band. Tony had a wonderful ear and could listen to a song then immediately pick out the chords and key. We always tried to sing in the original keys to get as close to recordings as possible. These days, you are almost apologetic if you say you are a cover band – but they were all the rage at the time. We updated our equipment in Geraldton with new amps – Harry, Bill and Tony all had double stacks and the back of the stage looked like a wall of amplifiers. We also got hold of a better PA system for the vocals and I bought a new drum kit.

As it drew time for our contract to end, we teed-up a gig at the Nookenburra Hotel in Perth where we became the resident band from Wednesdays through to the Sunday session. This was another extraordinary chapter in the band's history, as we never expected our act to be as popular in the city as it had been in the country. The crowds kept coming, especially on the weekends when we had to turn some people away – it was so packed. We did the floorshows that had been so successful up north and the crowds loved it. Bazz and I shared a unit nearby and that, of course, became the party pad, although we'd try to keep it quiet to avoid gatecrashers. I guess our neighbours got used to music playing until the early hours but if they complained, we'd invite them in and we never had any more trouble. Charm always works better than agro!

I'll talk more about the women in another chapter but suffice to add that they were around in numbers. My marriage was on the rocks and we were separated by this time, not surprisingly, and I do still harbour some guilt about the situation. To put it bluntly, I was a selfish bastard.

While we were working at 'The Nooky' as everyone called it, we were offered a contract to play at all the festivals in the nor'west. The offer was too tempting to refuse so we began making plans. We bought a small Dodge truck for the gear and decided to take a couple of cars too. The contract included the Spinifex Festival in Port Hedland, the Shinju-Matsuri (Pearl) Festival in Broome, the Boab Festival in Derby and the Cotton Festival in Kunnunurra.

Our final night at the Nooky was absolutely packed and it was quite sad to go but we did promise to play there again on our return.

*****

That trip north was exciting. All the festivals were memorable and distinct and everyone loved the band due to our versatility. We were invited to many homes and parties and were made quite a fuss of. In all the towns there was a real party atmosphere that we, of course, helped along. I think Derby was one of our favourite towns. We were billeted out in a couple of houses – Tony and I shared Marie and Ron Altham's home who turned out to be very relaxed hosts. Every night we had a Barbie and lots of beer and it was open house once we'd finished playing. We also got to know the young nurses at the Derby District Hospital and took them on a fun cruise on Lake Argyle at Kununura. All in all, it was a wonderful few weeks and once we'd completed the last festival at Kununarra, we headed up to Darwin for a stint there.

A bloke who ran a group of hotels offered us a season playing in four different venues – The Top of the Don, Fanny Bay, The Darwin and a hotel out at Nightsbridge. We were given rooms at the Fanny Bay, a lovely old hotel overlooking Fannie Bay that, sadly, was destroyed the following year (1974) during Cyclone Tracy. We were in Darwin late 1973 and all those houses on stilts were everywhere. Even then I thought them a bit flimsy for a big storm. The town had a magic atmosphere, it was very laid back and casual and we fitted in well. Everyone loved the band and all the venues were well patronised. I don't think we'd ever drunk so much beer! The huge 'Darwin Stubbies' were still available back then and once you'd downed a couple of those, there was not much else you could do, you were legless. The meals at the Fannie were excellent and we used to set off to the gigs with full bellies and a few glasses of wine under our belts.

I think we all ended up a bit 'troppo' as we sacked Bill, the lead guitarist, for arriving at gigs pissed out of his mind – but we were really not much better ourselves. We carried on as a four-piece and Bill's absence didn't seem to make that much difference. While we were playing one night at the Top of The Don, a bloke called Mick Kimpton approached us and asked if we'd like to do a month in Kununurra, to open the Ord River Sports Club. We agreed, and when our contract ran out, we made plans to head south. We drove down to Kununurra with the truck, Bazz's van and my old Ford Fairlane. The night before we left, a coconut fell down from a tree at the Fannie Bay and broke my windscreen! There was no time to replace it so we headed off with no windscreen, which was ok in the heat but not so good when we drove through a swarm of locusts. We had to abandon the car and let them fly right through it – when they'd passed, we got back in and drove on.

Kununurra was interesting. We played about four nights a week, I think, and on the days off we explored the area. Cotton farming was in vogue and huge areas of land were irrigated from the Ord River. Bazz and I took a couple of ladies out to a swimming hole for a picnic lunch one day and we all took a skinny dip in the afternoon. I climbed up naked onto some rocks just as a tourist bus arrived for a photo opportunity. The others fell about laughing in the water but I was well and truly caught out!

On a later outing, we found another swimming hole in the bush and we were surprised to find two bikini-clad girls sunning themselves on a large rock. I fell in love immediately with one of them and found that she was living and working in Wyndham as a nurse. I spent lots of driving time going back and forth between Wyndham and Kunnunurra to get to know this girl and we developed a strong relationship. She had a perfect figure and a sunny nature with a great sense of humour. I wonder where she is now?

The Ord River Sports Club became a focal point for the town and we had lots of fun playing for the locals, endeavouring to do all their requests. Tony and I stayed with the Kimptons who treated us very kindly, though I suspect they found some of our antics a bit alarming.

Those were great days. We would sail a little dinghy on the Ord River dam during the days or go for drives out into the bush.

One incredible gig was organised for us to go right out into the interior, just inside the Northern Territory border, on a station. We drove all day and arrived just on dusk to see this huge paddock covered with light aircraft. The party had been organised by the station owners and the bush telegraph had gone out to farmers all over Australia who jumped into their planes and flew in for the bash. Everyone was dressed in their finery – lovely ladies in long dresses, dripping with jewellery, and their gentleman farmers in formal dark suits with bow-ties. It was amazing and quite surreal out there miles from anywhere with the stars blazing overhead and the shearing shed decked out in bright lights and decorations. We didn't have to work too hard on that crowd – they were in party-mood the minute we began playing – stomping on the wooden shearing floor, causing heaps of dust to rise up and partly choke us.

I lost count of the beers and champagne we drank but the boys were well and truly pissed by the end of the night, all of us were too knackered to chat up the beautiful women whose husbands had passed-out.

The next morning, it was straight back into the champers before an enormous cooked breakfast out in the paddock. One by one the planes took off and we eventually left too for the long drive back to Kununurra. It had been a memorable gig. To this day, we don't know the name of the station, who the owners were or who was on the guest list – amazing!

The following year, the festival organisers flew us up to play at all the festivals again. That was quite a compliment for the band as we must have been a big hit with the locals.

*****

Rock 'n Roll days were coming to an end for me. Tony left the band when we got back to Perth and went off to join *The Rock 'n' Roll Show* (showband). Bazz and I got a band going with Peter Robbins from *Breakaway* but it never really fired. We called the band *The Soundell Revue* and did a few pub gigs but it was like being on autopilot after all the fun we had in the Haze. I reckon the band should have been called *"The Death Knell Revue"!* It didn't take long for the band to break up and Bazz and I went on to join *The Rock 'n' Roll Show* ourselves for a while.

It was a six-piece band with strong vocal harmonies and drew good crowds at the Morley Park Hotel.

I began a teaching degree around this time and found the late night band playing neither conducive to study or family life. The final straw for my decision to give up rock 'n' roll bands was the sheer volume of the music – so loud that even the drum kit had to be miked up.

I was offered a job in *The Storyville Jazzband,* a trad-jazz band playing around Perth, and I made the switch to jazz quite happily. I played with Storyville for around twenty years and there would be few venues around Perth the band hasn't performed at.

Storyville saw various members come and go, but the best line-up I can recall is Dixie Kidd (the leader) on the cornet, Bob Benton on trombone, Peter Groos on reeds, Alex de Fries on double bass, Graham Palmer on banjo and myself on drums. We had a driving sound and played some great arrangements of jazz standards. Dix was an excellent entertainer and vocalist and this helped make the band very popular. He did struggle with the odd (sic!) note on his cornet but his delivery was always so good that we forgave him (most of the time.) Quite often we would stitch Dix up. He loved telling long jokes so after he began a story, we would sneak off stage one by one and hide until the punch line then he'd turn round and say:

"Where are those bastards?" The audiences loved it.

The Storyville Jazzband – l to r: Pete, Graham, Dix, me, Bob and Alex

We played at the Como Hotel every afternoon on Saturday for 10 years, which was something of an achievement, but nothing compared to the *Cornerhouse Jazzband* who played regularly at the Railway Hotel in North Fremantle for over 37 years – and are still there. Must be a world record for the longest live music gig.

The trad jazz scene in Perth is a very close-knit community of musicians and we all work in different bands at times. I enjoyed playing in the hard driving *New Orleans Heritage Jazzband* for many years but eventually was replaced when we went off sailing. I'm back playing with them now – well into the 21st century and it's still good fun.

The New Orleans Heritage Jazzband

The best years in Storyville saw us as the first on band for two of the UK's most popular jazz bands – *Kenny Ball and his Jazzmen* and *Acker Bilk and the Paramount Jazzband*. Those were fabulous occasions for us and we loved it. Another worthwhile two weeks was when we had Pat Halcox, from *Chris Barber's Jazzband*, on trumpet with us for a series of gigs. It was very exciting musically and Pat's musicianship lifted the band to new heights.

Pat Halcox (from Chris Barber's Jazzband) playing with Storyville.

A jazz band gets to play at all sorts of venues and Storyville has played on the back of trucks, in the street, at most pubs around Perth, on large outdoor stages, over at Rottnest Island, at jazz festivals, in concert halls and on jetties and boats!

The Jazz Club of WA was formed in the early 80s to promote traditional jazz. The Club is still going and meets at the Yokine Bowling Club on Tuesday nights. It's good fun with a wide variety of bands. I might see you there.

I must mention one hilarious (but could have been frightening) gig. We were asked to play for a tavern in Redcliff along Great Eastern Highway. We set up the gear to an almost empty room and began playing. Soon there was a huge roar and dozens of bikies rode up and wandered in. They took one look at us and yelled, "Play some fucking rock'n'roll!" We just bashed on with jazz and tried to play something a bit rocky but they were not impressed. By this time the place was full – one big hairy bloke came right up to the stage and said to Dix, "Play fucking rock 'n' roll or I'll straighten your trumpet out!"

Bloody hell! We took a break and Dix went over to explain that we were a jazz band. When he told them that he had a motorbike and had recently fallen off and busted a leg (he still had a crutch), they were happy. For a while anyway – until the last set, when the alcohol took over and a huge punch up began. There must have been two gangs there and it was on! Glasses smashed, jugs banged on heads, blood and guts on the floor. It was scary but when Dix went to get the money, they stopped and let him through – then began again after he got back to the bandstand. Incredible! To top it all off, the manager said, "Would you boys like to come back next week!?" Five cops cars came up but not one cop came inside.

The York Jazz Festival was always the highlight of our year and it ran successfully for about ten years until political squabbles between various factions in the town killed it. The festival offered opportunities for local bands to gig and for us to enjoy inter-state and overseas bands and artists.

With bands playing on street corners, in pubs, marquees and the town hall, there was a tremendous atmosphere in the town. Most years we would go and stay for the weekend and the morning 'Jazz Breakfasts' with live music became my favourite part of this wonderful long weekend.

The original festival was the brainchild of Roy Burton, leader and trombone player with *The Cornerhouse Jazzband* and I'm sure that it would still be going were it not for the politics. It all began in a very amateurish way but ended up a very professionally run festival. I feel privileged to have been part of that festival over many years.

I still play the occasional trad jazz gig and really love the music – it's fun, toe-tapping and served up with a bit of humour, goes over well with audiences of all ages. Sadly, without a younger following, this art form will probably die as we're all getting older and young bands are not replacing us. There are some wonderfully talented young musicians in Perth but they seem to prefer more mainstream and modern jazz. Many great jazz musos have graduated from WAPA. I reckon a young band playing trad jazz with drive and excitement would ignite audiences fed mainly rap, hip-hop, heavy metal or head banging DJ stuff. Younger people do go to the Friday night Cellar in North Perth where *Cornerhouse* play but they don't seem to come along to other jazz venues.

Chapter Five

Working Life

"Work to live, don't live to work!" Anon

I look back on all the jobs I've had and I'm amazed at how easy it was to obtain work, even as a teenager. The first paid job I had was in the long summer school holidays when I was 14. Barry (the Rector's eldest son) and I approached the richest local farmer and asked him for a job. He said, "Yes, boys – you begin tomorrow!"

It was a laugh. Barry and I were both given a quick lesson on how to drive a tractor and then off we went. We had to muck-spread manure, plough large fields and rake fields after the crop had been harvested. We were allowed to drive the tractors home and I used to park mine in a field just near our house. We couldn't drive on the roads but all the fields (paddocks in Oz!) interconnected so it was easy to get home. My mother made up a lunch and thermos of tea and off I went at seven in the morning until late in the afternoon. We were paid £7 each – big money for 14 year olds back then. Other jobs included harvesting sugar beet and stacking bales of hay after the wheat had been harvested. Barry and I took turns driving for the harvesting job while the other stood on the baler. The bales came out onto a flat board and the farmhand had to stack them four high, then pull a lever and the stack would (hopefully!) drop off and remain upright. If you got it wrong, you had to jump off and stack the bales by hand while the driver waited. We soon got good at it.

An amusing incident happened when we were having lunch with one of the farmer's regular labourers. I'd just heard this joke, so I asked him, "How tall are you, Derek?"

He replied seriously, "About five foot eight."

To which I laughed, "Geez – I didn't know they piled shit that high!"

He went berserk and began thumping me like a madman. Barry dragged him off and luckily, I wasn't badly hurt. It was a lesson in humility for me. I hadn't realised until then how the villagers really viewed us privileged officer's kids.

The work lasted all holidays and we both earned a tidy sum. I put mine towards my first drum kit.

My next jobs were in London after I got back from Jordan and we formed *The Temeraires*. I took on various labouring and storeman positions and also worked as a budding camera technician for a while, as mentioned previously. I never really took the jobs seriously as all my energy went into the band. We thought we were going to make the big time! Lots of musicians in the '60's had high hopes and it was pure luck if you were talent spotted.

After I went back home to Suffolk, I worked in a canning factory in Woodbridge that was well paid, but pretty boring. I then got a job in Felixstowe in a factory that went for twenty-four hours a day. I think I was called a 'process' worker. There were no windows in that factory so it didn't make any difference what time of the day or night it was – you just kept plugging away at your machine like a bloody robot! I worked night shifts to make more money, but only lasted a few months. The 'process:'

1. Pick up metal triangle with left hand.

2. Lift machine guard, place triangle on the block.

3. Close guard, grab handle and pull down hard – 'clunk' – a hole appeared in the triangle.

4. Remove triangle with right hand and place it in a box. Repeat process all night – can you imagine it? And it was never explained what the component was needed for.

After the factory work, I thought I needed some fresh air so I applied to become a deckhand on a fishing trawler sailing out of Lowestoft. I was given a job immediately and all I had to do was buy some oilskins, a turtle-necked fisherman's woolly jumper, thigh length boots and I was ready for sea – so I thought.

Bloody hell! As soon as we cleared the harbour, it was straight into a heavy North Sea swell and the boat began to buck and plunge like mad. I was seasick and crept down below to my bunk to endure a horror I'll never forget. The mixture of vomit, fish and diesel fuel fumes had me gagging until nothing was left to come up except yellow bile. I was a cot case for three days. I eventually surfaced to begin work after a huge breakfast of fresh fish and bread – washed down with an enormous mug of hot tea.

My job as the 'deckie learner' was to shovel all the blood, guts and offal over the side after the gutting and cleaning of the catch. I quickly learnt how to gut and clean large cod, plaice, haddock and sole. The first time, I began to shovel the horrible mess over the *windward side* and the wind blew it back in my face and down the front of my oilies. It was awful but the skipper and crew loved it! By the time I'd finished cleaning up the mess after each haul and crawled back down to my bunk to get a bit of kip, I would just get off into a deep sleep when I would be roughly shaken awake again – "Up net, up net!" was the call. That happened every two and a half hours for ten days.

Once we'd landed our catch and filled the hold, it was back

to Lowestoft, but my job was never finished. I had to polish the brasses (portholes and any other brass objects on the boat) while my fellow crew mates were down below sleeping.

The money was good. I received £7 as a base wage and then took a percentage of the catch – making a total of about £20 or more a trip. That was pretty good in 1965.

The winter months were particularly hard. I remember we had to heave-to once for a day because it was too rough to fish. On another occasion, the net grabbed onto something on the seabed and we came to a juddering halt. Lots of wrecks from both world wars are scattered on the North Sea seabed. The net was pulled up and it was full of tears. We had to fix it on the spot and my job was to load up the 'needles' with thread and pass them to the skipper and mate. Being mid-winter, my hands were freezing, but we had to keep going – all the while the boat was broadside to the seas and rolling from gunwale to gunwale. I didn't have time to feel scared.

That was my last job in the UK before I emigrated to Australia on my own in 1966. I was 20.

*****

In Australia, the jobs continued to be easy to get. The first one I remember was as a builder's labourer in Surfer's Paradise, not far from Brisbane. I worked with a big blonde surfie guy and our first task was in Surfers – digging the foundations for a building in the main street.

"Hey, mate, you get on the banjo while I use the pick!"

"The banjo? But mate, I'm a drummer!"

"You stupid, Pom – the banjo is that shovel!"

It was hard work, but lots of laughs. The meter maids easily distracted us when they strolled past by to drop coins into expired parking meters. I just loved their golden bikinis and lovely tans. Turning to perve one time whilst using a jackhammer, I nearly fell off the scaffolding!

I have to admit I was a bit surprised when my all workmates (except the surfie) turned up for work in navy blue singlets and shorts, like a uniform. Each bloke also had a Gladstone Bag (the old Doctor's bag) with his lunch and a flask of coffee inside; the bags were never clipped shut, always hanging open. Was that to look cool? It cracked me up, especially when they asked,

"Has mum packed your lunch?"

I'd burst out laughing and say, "My mum is 12,000 miles way in England!" Apparently, it was ok to call your wife "mum" – very strange.

Actually for me and my mate, lunch was always a 2 litre coke and hot pie (with dead ' orse, of course!). That took some getting used to, as pork pies were served cold in the UK.

The labouring mate I had befriended after some months working in Brisbane pooled our money and we bought an old Holden and headed north to Cairns. My mate had a sister up there and we stayed with her for a while.

That trip up the coast was memorable as we were able to get work in every town we stopped in. I was earning about forty bucks or more a week and living well. There was labouring work on building sites, helping cane cutters, and fruit picking available. I spotted the first cruising yacht I'd seen in Australia anchored off Cairns and I thought to myself at the time,

"That looks good – I'd like to own one of those one day.".

It was a dream that eventually came true.

*****

After we returned to Brisbane, I decided to go west. Roger, my labourer mate, wanted to remain in Brisbane. I met another bloke in a youth hostel in Brissie and we decided that we'd hitchhike over to Perth. We set off just before Christmas 1966 and reached Melbourne for my 21st birthday on the 29th. We had a few dollars left and bought a flagon of cheap red wine – called 'plonk' by the Aussies. Well, I was a total mess for the whole of the next day. We slept in the botanical gardens in the centre of the city and I just lay under a tree for the whole day, trying to recover.

The next day we bussed out of the city and managed to get a lift to Adelaide. From Adelaide, we thumbed a ride to Ceduna and waited two days there for a lift right across the Nullabor. What a laugh! These two young guys picked us up in an old American V8 station wagon. The driver's window glass was missing and I had to lie across a 44-gallon drum of petrol in the back – as there were only a few places for getting petrol back in 1967. We set off for the west and all was ok until we ran out of bitumen, then it was into the finest bull dust and potholes for about 1000 km. With no driver's window, we were completely covered in dust and all you could see were our red eyeballs. We drove non-stop and topped up with fuel where we could. Sleep was just about impossible and we all took turns to drive. It was fun, though, and we laughed a lot. The old car just got us to a service station outside Perth when the motor finally died. One of the guys phoned his dad and he came and picked us up. They just left the car there.

We cleaned ourselves up at the family home, did our washing, and then looked for accommodation. We were offered free accommodation at a vicarage in Mosman Park, in return for doing some gardening and handyman jobs that needed attention.

From there, I found digs in Fremantle along Marine Terrace. This little old landlady rented her front room to me cheaply. She thought I was 'a nice boy.'

My first paid job in the west was as a 'roof carpenter' with a team of guys working out in the wheatbelt, putting temporary tin roofs on wheat silos. I had very little money - I had recently arrived in Perth with just ten cents before I could get to a bank. I spent that on a bottle of milk!

This job offered accommodation in caravans, as it travelled from town to town. That was great, but with no food supplied, I had to wait a week for my first payday to buy some groceries. The other workers were very reluctant to share their food so I was near starving by the end of the week. It was tough work too. We had to hammer lengths of wood into the wheat, then place timbers on top to support the corrugated sheets, which were held in place with twitching wire. Handling the hot tin was horrible and we worked almost waist deep in the wheat at times. It was January and very hot.

"Watch out for Joe Blakes!" warned the foreman.

"Who the bloody hell is he?" I asked naively.

"Snakes – you silly Pom!" he laughed.

Christ, what with the heat, lack of food, flies and now snakes, I was beginning to wonder if I should think about going back to the UK.

My first pay packet was a huge relief – I clearly remember buying bread, sardines, tinned salmon, baked beans and all I could lay my hands on after I paid back the food that I'd 'borrowed'.

The second trip was with a much better organised team. They had a cook's caravan as well as vans for the workers and it was relatively comfortable. We even had extra water for quick showers. I remember covering silos in many little towns and railway sidings out in the wheatbelt.

The strange names I remember like Bencubbin, Muckinbudin and Nungarin fascinated me and still do.

My next foray into the West Australian workforce was working for the Agricultural Department. The first job entailed grading and testing wool samples. It was nice easy work, not well paid but you ended the day with soft hands.

The second job offered to me by the Agricultural Department involved spraying for argentine ants all round the metro area. I was given a Land Rover with a tray on the back. On the tray was a large tank of water, hoses, drums of dieldrin and the spraying equipment. Deildrin is a horrible, very environmentally unfriendly poison to kill the ants with. I had no idea of this at the time in late '67.

I was given a young guy (I was only 21!) as an offsider. He was such a slow worker that we christened him *Cyclone* – I was beginning to get the hang of Aussie humour.

I recall having to spray all round Lake Monger with this horrid poison. Cyclone would walk behind the Land Rover spraying while I drove in low gear at walking pace. I'd give him a spell when he looked suitably knackered, then he'd drive for a while. At the end of the day we were instructed to tip out any leftover poison and clean the tank with water before heading back to the depot. I have to confess that on more than one occasion, we tipped the stuff into a creek. I feel awful about it now.

Argentine ants did originate from Argentina. They are tiny, but very aggressive and can get in anywhere. The boss showed me a jar with a screw-top lid and inside were ants devouring some panty hose – that's how determined they were. He'd been given the jar by a house owner who's home was being invaded by them. I don't hear of them being a problem now so maybe that terrible dieldrin did help eradicate them.

Further jobs involved being a storeman for a polishing and cleaning product manufacturer in Rivervale, Peerless Emulsion. I worked my way up to being in charge of the whole production and distribution side of the factory until I headed north to play music. I was a married man by this time.

Other jobs I had were as a delivery driver for Mazda spare parts, a spare parts man for Coventry Motor Replacements and

Tisco '94, a company that specialised in auto/marine instruments. Around this time I saw an ad in the weekend paper that was about mature age entry into teaching.

I thought I'd done enough semi-skilled jobs to last a lifetime so I applied. I had to write an essay, do an IQ test and attend an interview with a superintendent. It was all pretty easy and I was accepted as a student at Graylands Teachers' College in 1976.

It was fun at teacher's college. We 'mature age students' (I was only 31 when I entered) used to annoy the kids straight out of high school by asking the lecturers lots of probing questions. The lecturers loved the discussions but the young budding teachers thought we were boring. I loved the academic experience and enjoyed researching for the assignments. We 'oldies' took all the top marks and prizes. I won a pair of Henry Lawson poetry books for an essay I wrote. I also helped edit and compile articles for *The Klaxon,* the Graylands student paper. Some were quite controversial and I'm convinced that I only received a 'C' for physical education because we took the micky out of their department in one article. My final SWA (Semester weighted average) was 73.5% – that was because I'd upset the Phys Ed dept. Otherwise, I'd have received a Diploma of Distinction (75%).

My old school teachers would have been surprised and very pleased as I could, *'Do better when I tried!'*

Not long before we completed our training, two rooky teachers who were ex-SAS soldiers persuaded about ten of us to do a skydive. Another stupid decision – I don't think I've ever been so scared. We did some training: jumping off tables and things and learning how to bend our knees and roll over on impact with the ground. The big day came at a dirt airfield off the Brookton Highway. A little single-engined plane was waiting for us – with its door off! We climbed into overalls, strapped on the parachutes and got in. The plane roared off down the dirt runway and climbed into the sky. Our SAS instructor had us all hooked on a 'static line' which would open the 'chute if you panicked and forgot to pull the ripcord. One by one, we climbed out of the open door, one foot on a landing wheel, and both hands grabbing the wing strut. Looking back at the instructor, he then gave you the thumbs up and you let go! Shit! I fell backwards, yelling, "Fuuuuuuck!" as loud as I could, then 'whumph' the 'chute was dragged open. What a fantastic feeling – so peaceful after the roar on the plane. Two other students jumped after me and headed down. I seemed to float up – and then realised I had been caught in a thermal. I had quite a long descent and the relief of the parachute opening was so great that I spewed up in mid-air. I landed ok, bent my knees and rolled over but was dragged along the ground until I could deflate the 'chute. What an experience! Never did it again. One student hit the ground with his feet pointing down instead of flat – he received a broken ankle for forgetting his training.

I graduated after four years. I had to take a year off to work as a delivery driver to save some money as the student allowance was not enough to live on with a young family. I was also still doing gigs on the weekends in *The Rock 'n' Roll Showband*.

My first teaching job was at Calista Primary School with a year six class. The kids were pretty good and we did lots of interesting stuff together. My assembly items were loved by the parents and kids – I guess I had a bit of flair for drama. One kid, Jason Flutter, was a space nut and he loved being Dr Who – with a whole cardboard control box that had lots of flashing lights on it. It was the highlight of his schooling. In my third year at the school, I took on a drama specialist role that involved taking classes from year one to year seven. It was quite demanding. With parent help, we turned a disused classroom into a mini-theatre and thus began the 'Calista Children's Theatre'.

We put on a pantomime at the end of the year. I wrote up a script for Aladdin and the kids acted very well and made it a huge success. Some of the naughtiest kids in year seven were given parts to play and proved to be great contributors. They were great in the show and developed a love of entertaining. They never gave me any trouble as I had other kids just dying to take their places if they mucked up – very good motivation.

Calista was a fairly challenging school and I thought my next appointment would be a doddle. How wrong I was! The next school was Hainsworth Primary in Girrawheen and I was shocked at the behaviour and attitude of the year six kids I was given. They were so angry and aggressive to each other, and to me. I would get to school after the weekend and find broken windows, urine on the carpet and faeces rubbed on the blackboard. After a few weeks I still hadn't managed to get through to the class so I rang the superintendent and asked him to move me to another school, or I'd resign.

He told me to take a few days off and he'd see what he could do. Superintendents carried a lot of power and influence in those days – some teachers feared them but I always thought they helped keep academic standards up and were really helpful with professional advice. I felt a sense of failure with that class but I'd done my best.

He rang after about a week and said, "Get yourself over to Illawarra Primary at Ballajura, they have a class for you."

Thus began the best ten years of my teaching career. My first class was a delightful bunch of year threes and we had lots of fun together. There was a pair of twins in the class, Brione and Fiona who were so creative, always keeping me on my toes in every lesson. In my second year there I began a radio station with some of the year seven kids. We called it Radio 6IW and it became a huge success. Every Friday afternoon the whole school would tune in and listen to musical requests, gossip, quizzes, stories and games. We often had guests along to interview and the kids became very professional at working out appropriate questions to ask. We even had ex-premier, Brian Burke, on one afternoon. He was very entertaining and thought the kids were really good.

A team of my 6IW kids were chosen to help promote Radio Lollipop at PMH (Princess Margaret Hospital for Children). They put on a show there and had an interesting time interviewing sick kids, playing games and playing requests. They had the opportunity to interview the then health minister, Mr Barry Hodge, as well. Kiss was a favourite band with primary kids in the 80s and the kids had lots of requests for their songs.

Two of my Radio 6IW kids interviewing Barry Hodge, then WA minister for health. We were helping promote Radio Lollipop at PMH.

I was entering my forties and it was a very creative stage of my life. Every class was different and I really enjoyed my ten years at Illawarra. Radio 6IW continued on long after I left the school, enjoying popularity with the kids for over twenty years

– surely something of a record for a school project?

I transferred to Joondalup Primary and that was enjoyable too but lacked the dynamic and cohesive staff of Illawarra. There were more egos and competition amongst the staff but we still had an enjoyable time. One principal, Joe, loved assemblies and they became something of a community event with elaborate items from students and staff and 'on the spot' quizzes. I always brought jazz bands along to my schools to play at concerts and assemblies. We musos love playing for very enthusiastic young audiences.

I did a stint as a music specialist at Joondalup and had all the kids learning rudimentary drumming. I had the kit set up in the music room and let the best-behaved kid have a thrash on the drums at the end of the lesson. It was a great motivator. I also did a stint as deputy principal and found that very interesting.

Another worthwhile project was the HF radio link-up we had with the school when Aileen and I sailed to Cocos (Keeling). We arranged a daily sked through Telstra and the kids plotted our position on a large chart, noting any sea life or birdlife we'd seen and forecasting the daily run (or distance sailed). That was fascinating for them.

When I turned 55, I retired from full-time teaching but kept on with relief teaching and short-term contracts. I moved up into high school and really found it more stimulating. What mostly made my mind up to retire was the advent of 'student outcomes' and the emphasis on 'open learning'. I was a bit of a traditionalist and loved teaching the basics. In my twenty-one years as a primary classroom teacher, I always drilled tables, mental arithmetic, spelling, punctuation, grammar and 'running writing' and I hated kids leaving at the end of the year if they didn't have a pretty good grasp of most of them. General knowledge was another passion and I loved playing quiz games with the kids. When I see the standard of work of some of the kids now, I'm horrified at their lack of general knowledge and some of their low literacy and numeracy skills. I could never see anything wrong with rote learning as, to me, once you'd got your basics together, then you could become creative or move onto higher maths.

The analogy I always quoted at staff meetings and seminars was that all of us want to be able to drive a car and you go along to be *taught* how. Those that want to know more about what's under the bonnet can go and do an engineering course – but we all need to be able to drive. To me, education was a bit the same and kids needed to be taught and drilled in the basics. There is a bit of a drive to go 'back to basics' now – how the wheel has turned. The emphasis is on DI (direct instruction) which is a bit like rote learning, with the teacher leading with direct, explicit instructions and the kids following up what's been learnt.

Chapter Six

Sailing Years

"I wanted freedom, open air and adventure. I found it on the sea."
                                            Alain Gerbault

Sailing has always been a big part of my life. It began at the high school in Germany which was built around a large lake, as mentioned earlier. The boat shed had cadet and pirate dinghies and a couple of jolly boats.

The cadets were tiny and carried a crew of two, the pirates carried three and the left-over kids and novices went out in the jolly boats. I started off in the jolly boats. They were a bit scary as they'd heel right over in a gust and water would slop up through the centre-board casing – one poor unfortunate boy was always on baling duty down in the bilges. Being gaff rigged with heavy spars, gybing was dangerous, and how one of us kids wasn't hurt or killed is a miracle – duty of care? I don't think the phrase was invented back then. It was a relief to get into a cadet dinghy as a for'ard hand. My job was to trim the headsail, or jib, and provide ballast and balance for the skipper who steered and trimmed the mainsail. It was great sport and we had mini races between the boats. Cadets were easily capsized and we boys often ended up in the chilly lake water, but not for long as we soon learned to right the boats quickly.

I forgot about sailing for a long time after school but my

interest was sparked again when I saw that yacht in Cairns in 1966. It took until 1975 before I was in a position to purchase a little yacht but once I was back on the water, I never looked back and ended up owning ten yachts over thirty-four years. The most memorable years on the water were the times I lived on board and cruised overseas – once with Aileen and the first time on my own.

I began in Perth with sailing lessons on the Swan River, sailing a GP 14 dinghy. From there, I bought a 17-foot Red Jacket and cruised about the river with my young family, even venturing over to Rotto with our little girls bundled up down below in the tiny cuddy cabin. I began racing at Perth Flying Squadron Yacht Club (PFSYC) and by 1984 was winning some races in my 20-footer. Eventually that yacht was a bit small and had no head (toilet) so we moved up into a 24-foot Spacesailer. She was fun to sail and I even got as far as division 4 champion one year but by now I was becoming a bit bored with sailing round the buoys, and became more interested in cruising.

I looked around for a yacht which would take me ocean cruising and found a Duncanson 29, a lovely South Australian design with a longish keel for stability. She looked sleek and business like. We sailed her up to Sorrento Quay (Hillarys Boat Harbour) and rented a pen in the public marina. The urge to sail further afield was growing in me and plans were made to sail across the Indian Ocean. I guess the urge came from all the cruising books I'd read over many years. Authors like Chichester, Moitessier, Knox-Johnson, John Wray (a Kiwi), Kay Cottee, Jon Sanders and others had really sparked my imagination and I just felt I had to give it a go.

Having few navigational skills, both Aileen and myself enrolled in Fremantle TAFE for classes. I did coastal, offshore and ocean (celestial) navigation and earned a Diploma in Nautical Science. I talk about Aileen's work later.

Learning Celestial Navigation

In 1990 I set off for South Africa in the little 29-foot Duncanson sloop – she was a terrific choice, being a boat that handled the seas better than I did at times! I have written about this trip in my first book, *Lotus 11 – an Indian Ocean Adventure* which is still available through the library services. I'll mention here that we called in at the Indian Ocean islands of Cocos (Keeling), Rodregues, Mauritius and La Reunion and eventually made landfall in Durban, South Africa. Those tropical islands were all gorgeous, each having different characteristics and I'm very lucky to have anchored at them in my own little home on the seas.

Lotus 11 – a very safe little 29-footer

This was a dream realised and reality stacked up to my imaginative thinking and dreaming about what the trip would be like. *Lotus 11*, being a small boat, attracted attention wherever she went and this gained us lots of invites to dinner and onto other cruising yachts. In 1990 it was not really expensive and I only spent eight thousand dollars that included a side trip by air to England and Rome, to meet up with Aileen. The cruising lifestyle is really appealing but these days you would need a lot more money to do it in reasonable comfort.

People were so friendly and would keep asking, "How did you do it in that little boat?"

As I said, the boat handled the seas well and looked after me, even when I sailed her single-handed back to Fremantle from Durban. That took me fifty one days of *complete solitude* – no radio contact, no satellite phone, no email, no Facebook, no Twitter. I was completely on my own but didn't really feel lonely. After a horrible gale at the beginning of the voyage that lasted nearly three days and pushed me sixty miles north of Durban, I was seasick for almost two weeks. That gale blew up to 50 knots with 30-foot seas and was very scary in the little 29-footer. She would ride up, up, up the waves, heel right over at the top, then slide down the back of the seas.

I only recovered from the spewing with the help of Him Upstairs. I had taken Stugeron seasickness tablets but they were useless and I just spewed them up. In complete desperation, I thought I'd end it all by strangling myself with my safety harness but could not quite bring myself to do it. I cried out, "Dear God, please help me." You may believe this or not, but a loud voice in my head said, 'TAKE THE STUGERON!' I was sceptical, as the pills had done no good at all, but I took two and lay down on the cabin sole (floor) and went to sleep. When I awoke, the seasickness had gone and never came back for the rest of the voyage. It was amazing – and I'll give credit to Him Upstairs for helping me in my hour of need. I think we all call on His help when things get really bad.

Once I had recovered and got my sea legs back I really enjoyed my time at sea and felt at one with nature. I knew the sea could destroy me easily but I just surrendered to my circumstances and did my best to keep the boat moving. To me, the sea is like a heavy-weight boxer, you keep out of his way and go with the punches. The sea can destroy a little yacht anytime so you do have to work with it; always reef early in any sign of bad weather. I have discussed handling gales at sea in an article for *'Cruising Helmsman'* magazine (for those interested: Google, *"Handling a Gale at Sea" by Nigel Ridgway*). I became WA correspondent for that magazine for twenty years, writing articles on yachts, product reviews, destination pieces and our own adventures. It was an interesting part-time gig.

Me with Jeff (crew) at Cocos – a long way from home!

Sailing across the Southern Ocean, I befriended an albatross that stayed with me for two thousand miles. He would soar and glide round the boat everyday and I knew he was the same one as he had a chip out of one wing tip. As the sun set, he would land on the water ahead of *Lotus* and tuck his head under his wing to go to sleep. As I sailed past, he'd wake up and fly off ahead of the boat and do that again all night because he was there until the early hours of the morning, then he'd fly away for the whole day. As I began to head more north east to fetch Fremantle, he lost interest and I never saw him again but I've always remembered him. That voyage had a profound effect on me and helped make me realise what an amazing planet we live on. The seas go about their business unencumbered by us and provide so much for our planet. If we end up completely polluting the oceans – we only have ourselves to blame. In 1990 I saw no signs of pollution in the Southern and Indian Oceans. In mid-ocean, the colour of the sea is cobalt blue and it was mesmerising to gaze into its depths. The sea is alive with little creatures flitting around, some of which attach themselves to your hull! It was a very fulfilling experience to be 'Master and Commander' of my own little vessel and make all decisions. My life was in my own hands (and in the hands of Him Upstairs – sailors are naturally very superstitious).

The next voyage was eight years later when Aileen, myself and a friend, John, sailed our old wooden ketch, *Clare* to Cocos (Keeling). It took fourteen days (two days longer than *Lotus* – and the ketch was a 40-footer) but we had a great time with lots of laughs. What stands out in my mind on that trip was the daily HF radio sked with the kids back at Joondalup Primary and catching two large dorado, or dolphin fish. It felt quite cruel bringing them on board as they had lovely colours in the sea – silver, green and gold flashes pulsating through their terrified bodies. Once dispatched, they looked grey to me but they were lovely eating. One fish fed the three of us with large fillets for three days. Aileen had a lot of fun cooking them up in the galley. She served them with mashed potato and lovely Geraldton tomatoes. One experience I recall is sitting on the aft cabin top watching a full moon rise above the long swells behind us. I was on watch, Aileen and John were down below sleeping, and the moonlight shimmering on the waves was magical as the old girl ambled along at five knots.

Clare – our lovely vintage wooden ketch

When the sea is in a benign mood, she brings an incredible feeling of peace and tranquillity to one's psyche – just the opposite in a gale, when worry and apprehension take over. I found the sea had a great influence on my emotions and highs and lows were magnified compared to shore life. Aileen and John would agree with me on that point.

Aileen at sea catches up with her log book

That voyage had a sad ending as we ending up selling *Clare* to the Cocos island nurse and her mechanic boyfriend. Somehow, salt water had got into the engine, seizing the motor and there was no way I could fix it. Direction Island is a beautiful, calm anchorage and we were perplexed at how it happened. We suspected a very strange Aussie girl who'd been stuck at Cocos for 18 months, alone on her yacht. She had gone troppo and was quite disturbed. She would come over to our boat to demand beers in the afternoon (the ex-pats on West island refused to sell her any). If we gave her just one, she would become very abusive and angry. We thought that she might have climbed aboard when we were over at West Island and poured water into the air intake – but we couldn't prove it. We'd had *Clare* for seven years and had sailed her in some very rough seas and never had any trouble with seawater getting into the engine. A mystery we'll never solve. The couple that bought her eventually fixed the motor and sailed away on their own adventures.

Our third big trip was to sail yet another of our yachts from Hillarys Yacht Club round the top to Queensland and on to Coffs Harbour in NSW. This was about two thirds of an Australian circumnavigation and took us almost two years. It was a retirement project many years in the planning. The yacht we completed this voyage in was an NZ built 39-footer, sloop-rigged and very comfortable to live on. Her name was *Toroa* which is Maori for 'wandering albatross' – very fitting.

Toroa – a Kiwi built 39-footer.
Lovely to sail and live aboard

On 3rd May 2001 we departed the yacht club and sailed straight through to Jurien Bay; an overnighter of 100nm (or about 200kms.) We rode out a 45 knot gale in the harbour but that was the worst gale we encountered as the weather improved and became warmer as we made our way north. We explored Shark Bay, the Ningaloo Reef, the Pilbara coast, and arrived in Broome on June 30th.

Broome is not easy for visiting yachts. We anchored off Cable Beach near Gantheum Point, behind the reef, but it was rolly in any NW breeze. With such a huge tidal range (10 m), it was a big job to get the dinghy ashore through the break on the beach and we always got wet bums! Luckily, we had fold-down wheels on the back of the rubber ducky, so we could haul it up the beach at high tide, then drag it over the sand at low tide when we got back from town. Low tide seemed to coincide with afternoons. One night it was particularly rolly so we upped anchor and motored round to Roebuck Bay where it was much more comfortable.

A big scare had occurred a day out of Broome: lots of vibration and noise was coming from the engine room. I pulled up the cover and found the whole engine and gearbox moving about horribly. One of the gearbox universal joints had failed (the engine was installed back to front and the prop shaft was driven through a 4-wheel drive transfer box). Bloody frightening! I had to shut down the motor and we sailed into Gantheum Bay very gingerly. We found a spare parts shop and bought another uni joint. John helped with that job. John and Julie were sailing in tandem with us on their yacht, *Ulah*. That was very fortunate as John is a great mechanic and helped us three times before we eventually repaired and replaced the transfer box mountings completely at Lizard Island, after we fetched Queensland.

The six weeks we explored the Kimberley were quite

extraordinary. Everyday we had to work out tidal heights and currents in order to arrive at the next anchorage safely, with enough water under the yacht at low tide so we didn't hit the bottom. Aileen and I worked the navigation together, always double checking each other's work before we were satisfied. It is very important to work the tides and currents – it saves lots of diesel fuel and you can sail more efficiently if you have the current pushing you along – like a magic carpet ride. One highlight was the anchorage up Crocodile Creek.

Now, to get into this anchorage, you have to wait for a good high tide – we needed a least 2.5m, leaving a margin of 70cms under the keel (1.8m) – to go over the bar. Once inside, the water is reasonably deep all the way to the pool where we intended to tie-up to the rocks. It's about 5 nm up the creek, with a few twists and turns, motoring past the mangroves and cliffs. Around the final bend there's the pool with a waterfall cascading down the cliff – magic! We were in company with our friends John and Julie on *Ulah*. There's only room for two decent-sized yachts to anchor. We dug the bow anchors in, backed up to the waterfall and secured the stern lines to the rocks. Then we launched our dinghies to tie off springers either side, making things very secure. There was a ladder attached to the rocks right behind us and at high tide we could clamber up a couple of rungs to bring us to the lower pool – which was mostly fresh water. Spring tides enter the lower pool and the occasional croc drifts in too – hence the name. There are two other pools higher up the rocks and the top pool is right on the level of the surrounding plains which is perfect for skinny dipping, doing your ablutions and washing hair. There wasn't a soul around; just the roar of the waterfall and constant buzz of circadas.

Low tide was a complete shock! The whole anchorage drains out and we were left with a little pool just big enough for our boats and only a couple of meters of water under us. Where we'd come in was completely dry and the rocks, boulders and sand looked hazardous. No way could you get in on a low tide.

At the lower pool, yachties have left 'visiting cards' in the form of carvings, plastic lids, plates and so on with the yacht names and dates of arrival. We added ours.

We spent a magic five days in the Creek and had it all to ourselves except when a bunch of tourists came in from the Kimberley cruising vessel, *True North*. They were quite amazed to see two cruising yachts anchored up there.

Another scary part of the voyage was through what is called, 'The Gutter' on the chart. This is a very narrow gap at the northern end of Koolan Island. The current is compressed through this gap and then takes a fairly sharp turn so you have to be in complete control of the yacht as you get spun out of the gutter like a cork out of a champagne bottle. Quite unnerving.

I have to mention Honeymoon Bay. This is a quiet anchorage that is popular with 4-wheel drive owners and back-packers, who camp on the beach. It's not far from Kalumburu on a very dodgy dirt road. The place is managed by an aboriginal guy called Les French. He has a brick and tile residence on the beach but prefers to live in his humpy nearby. He said that his bay was very safe.

"There's no crocs in my bay!"

How wrong he was.

The second night there, we left our inflatable dinghy on its painter, hanging off the back of our boat. We were asleep when, about 11.20, we heard a splashing and thrashing behind us. I rose quickly, grabbed a torch, and rushed to the stern. There, a huge croc was trying desperately to flip our dinghy over! It was barrel-rolling, thrashing about and grunting. When I shone the torch in his eyes, he let go of the dinghy and sunk below the surface. Without thinking, I stepped down onto our duckboard, which was at water level and pulled the dinghy in to secure it on the davits. The shock hit and I began shaking as I realised how dangerous it was. We called out to John and Julie on *Ulah*. They appeared on deck and John shone a spotlight over the water between our boats – he picked out two sets of red eyes!

We made lots of noise and the crocs disappeared. We went back to bed, our ship's cat Chanelle, lying between us. After about half an hour, there were lots of thumps on the hull – we were scared stiff, lying there frozen with fear. Evenually, the thumping stopped as the crocs gave up and we got some fitful sleep.

The next morning, Les came over in his dinghy – "I've never seen a croc in my bay," he lied.

Our dinghy was ruined. The croc had bitten large holes in it. Repair patches were out of the question.

The amazing end to this story is that a catamaran sailed into the bay later in the day. They listened to our story and then offered to lend us their inflatable until we fetched Darwin seeing they had an aluminium dinghy as well – sailors helping each other out – incredible as we'd only just met.

By the way, the insurance company refused to replace the dinghy. It had to be trucked down to Perth from Darwin to be repaired. When it came back to Darwin, the guys in the depot cracked up as the consignment note stated (in big letters) NIGEL RIDGWAY – CROCODILE HUNTER EXTRORDINARE!!

Well, we can't leave the Kimberley without describing King George River. What an amazing experience that was. Not an easy gorge to get into. After battling our way against strong headwinds to get into the bay, we anchored overnight and next morning launched our dinghies (we were still sailing in tandem with *Ulah*). John and I took soundings and worked out a way in

– dropping off plastic bottles attached to fishing line with weights on to mark our passage. Late afternoon the tide was right and we slowly motored our way in, watching the depth sounder wavering with about 20cms under our keels! Once in the main river it was fantastic. It was deep. The gorge is lined with ancient rock formations in beautiful colours and rises to 90 meters either side. The colours vary from cream through all the oranges to browns and black. There's waterfalls, flowers and trees clinging to the sheer cliffs. Absolute magic! When we arrived at the end, we faced two sheer cliffs with waterfalls cascading down from the top. We anchored near the one with the most impressive fall, turned off the engines and sat spellbound. No one else there but us and *Ulahs*. We spent five days up there. We climbed up to the top of the cliffs for a look-see and were surprised to see the land was quite flat and stretched off into the distance as far as the eye could see. I guess the gorges were made after the last ice-age, heating and cooling causing the fissures in the land.

One evening we were treated to an amazing sight. Just after sundown (it gets pitch dark early with no moon) we were on deck chatting to *Ulahs* nearby when we saw this snake of lights in the water, heading for our boats. It turned out to be thousands of small fish and the lights were caused by bio-luminessence – a little understood phenomenon of some fish species. They parted at our bow and swam down either side of our yachts. This lasted for about forty minutes and we were gobsmacked. Looking back, I think how lucky we were to experience this lifestyle. The boat was our home; it was comfortable and we had most mod cons – we could even have 240v power provided by an alternator attached to the diesel motor. This ran the fridge, heated the water for showers and drove a desalinator so we could produce 2x 10 litres of fresh water everyday and often have enough left to give *Ulahs* a drum.

Toroa's very comfortable saloon – like a gypsy caravan!

Aileen and Chanelle fishing in King George River, Kimberley

Sailing across the Top End was interesting. There are not too many good anchorages and sometimes we just dropped the pick in the Timor Sea. One fascinating place was Port Essington on the Gulag Peninsula. Here we could motor sail right down into the bay and find the remains of an early British settlement at Minto Head. We anchored and went ashore. It was one of the saddest places we visited over the whole two years. A small British garrison was built here in 1838 and lasted just eleven years until 1849. The purpose was to claim the north of the continent before the French could but it was a disaster. Poor soil quality, malaria, starvation and an inability to use native help and knowledge eventually claimed all lives. The remains of the settlement can be seen – all that's left of the buildings are the chimneys, a few stone walls and some graves. The old 'Can Do' approach of the Victorians failed in this venture.

Interestingly, the Aboriginal tribes there were not hostile and tried to teach the Brits to trade with the Macassan fisherman who sailed down from Indonesia to trade with the natives, swapping clothes and weapons for beche de mer (sea slugs). This is a pretty much unacknowledged part of Australian history.

*****

Rounding Cape York Peninsula was exciting, which we did after crossing the Gulf of Carpenteria. That can be a notoriously difficult stretch of water, especially going west to east, punching into the sou'easterly breezes. Yachties call it the 'Gulf of Hysteria!'

Highs in the Great Australian Bight can cause very strong east/south easterly winds across the top of our vast continent. Sailors have to work the winds, tidal flows and currents to get the best passage making. That's quite an exercise in patience if you don't want to get bashed about by the seas.

We battled sou'easters all down the Queensland coast but made good progress when we got it right. Lizard Island was most interesting. This was the island where Lt James Cook found his way out of the Great Barrier Reef. After his charting and 'discovery 'of the east coast, as he made his way north inside the reef, he began to worry that the reef would come to a dead end and *Endeavour* would be trapped, unable to sail back south against the breeze. He anchored at Lizard Island (so called because of all the lizards they found) and climbed to the top of the hill where he could see there was a way out of the reef complex.

Well, we anchored there too and climbed the hill, now known as Cook's Lookout. Very tiring in the heat but worth the views and the signing of the visitors' book at the summit. The best bit was there right next to our yachts – a coral garden we could dive on and explore everyday in warm, clear water. Wonderful! All sorts of colourful fish swam around and giant clams of purple, green and yellow waited open-mouthed to grab some food (or your leg if you were stupid enough to tread on one!) Ashore, there's an expensive resort where the rich and famous love to holiday, but out of bounds to us scruffy yachties, of course. We could get a drink at the staff bar, which was something, I guess. Perhaps the most interesting feature on the island is the Marine Biology Laboratory facility where they conduct research for the Great Barrier Reef and carry out experiments. Students, professors, PhDs and marine biologists from all over the world compete to get there to do research, no wonder, as it is little short of paradise. We were shown around at no cost – fascinating. One German PhD student showed us these tiny little fingerlings swimming against a current of water from a pump. Her thesis was going to prove that when fish are spawned, they don't just float away on the ocean currents on the Barrier Reef, but can swim quite strongly against the flow and thus grow up in their own familiar patch of coral.

Queensland is an exciting coast to sail as it has so many excellent anchorages and islands, whereas, here on our Wild West coast, there are few safe havens.

We made our way down to Cairns and picked up our grandson, Adam. He was sixteen at the time. What a wonderful two weeks he had on board as we cruised south with him to Townsville. He is an amazing fisherman and I reckon he could catch a fish in a puddle! While he was on board, we had fish for dinner every night.

After a stay in Townsville, our next goal was the Whitsundays as we'd heard so much about them. There are 75 islands in the group and many of them have safe anchorages, making it one of the great cruising grounds of the world. We spent six months there exploring it all. Many people charter yachts in the Whitsundays and it was fun listening to the radio chit-chat as novices called up base complaining of flat batteries, dragging anchors and blocked toilets! It happened every day.

I was lucky to get a teaching contract for six weeks at Proserpine Senior High taking English classes. We anchored near the Whitsunday Yacht Club and Aileen would drop me ashore in the dinghy to go to work. One of the other teachers picked me up. Needless to say, much of my teaching involved telling the kids about our adventures – they loved it.

Two more very dangerous events occurred further south. We anchored in Bum's Bay, Southport, for a while after being tied-up to the mooring pontoons for yachties in the Brisbane River. That was a very rewarding experience. The mooring posts are opposite the botanical gardens and near the centre of the city. All we had to do was dinghy over to a little jetty, tie-up and then catch the free bus into the heart of Brisbane. It was wonderful, especially at night with all the city lights. But back to Bum's Bay. It was getting on for the change of season and summer thunderstorms. One afternoon, the sky looked really ugly, black with a horrible greenish tinge to it when, suddenly, it struck with real force: 60 knots of breeze, lightning and thunder. Aileen was down below doing something in the sink when *Bang*! a bolt hit the mast, flew into the water (down a chain I had attached to the mast as a conductor) and fizzed around Toroa. Bloody frightening – it took out our two main radios, the VHF and HF and other electrics. What really scared me (I was out in the cockpit) was that Aileen had her hands in water in the stainless steel sink. It could have taken her life. Funnily enough, the chart light had never worked, but in this strike it lit up brightly and stayed that way for a while and then died forever!

The second awful fright occurred up the Ballina River. Many of the NSW rivers have sand bars to cross before you can get up river. It's a tricky art to get the timing right – if the tide's coming out (ebbing) and there is some swell about, the waves can break dangerously and many yachts and power boats have come a cropper, often with loss of life. We stooged about for a while until we saw the waves dropping as the outflow eased, then motorsailed in very gingerly. We got in ok and moved up river opposite the town. After a couple of days, we saw that same sky again – blue/black clouds racing towards the town. *Bang*! 73 knots of wind, the anchor chain out straight like a rod, the dinghy out the back on its painter, up in the air, spinning! Bloody hell – I was in the middle of changing the oil and fuel filters and Aileen was down below again. The force of the wind knocked us over onto our beam ends – Aileen was looking down into the water through the saloon windows, books and stuff flying everywhere. In the cockpit, the water came up over the gunwale but soon cleared out through the drains. We were both very shaken.

We could not get the radios fixed in Ballina so sailed down to Coffs Harbour with our niece, Carolyn, on board. It was not a happy trip. The weather was pretty grim so we plugged on through the night, the jib slamming back and forth with the roll of the ship and it was a relief to get back into a pen at Coff's in the morning.

It was here that we decided to end our voyage. We'd had two good years but there were lots of jobs to do on the boat. Aileen flew home with Chanelle, our sea cat, and I booked a truck to take *Toroa* back to WA. That was very interesting. The truckie let me sleep on *Toroa,* so I went with him and spent five days getting to Mandurah. It was enjoyable, except for the tyre blowouts we had. People were amazed to see a pretty big 39-foot yacht on the trailer. Fortunately, we had a pen organised at Mandurah Offshore Fishing and Sailing Club, and after stepping the mast, we motored into the pen and lived on board while Aileen helped design our new house. It had been an incredible experience and we feel very fortunate to have had the privilege to do it and get home safely. Some of our friends never returned from their cruises and were lost at sea.

Footnote: We are always asked about our sea cat, Chanelle. She was a lovely companion on board and loved joining in with the fishing. Ragdolls are great talkers and she would 'meow' loudly when we returned to the ship – climbing down the steps to greet us. Sadly, she could not get used to life ashore and developed a urinary tract disease. We had to let her go eventually. We were so sad as she'd been with us through all the highs and lows of the cruise.

The Real Skipper – ship's cat Chanelle

Chapter Seven

Emigrating to Australia

"It was the bargain of the century – to sail aboard a cruise ship for a sum of just ten pounds!" A ship's officer

So how did I get to Australia? Well, I was at a bit of a loss after the break up of the *Temeraires* in London. I was back at home doing factory work wondering what to do next when I saw an ad about Australia in the local paper. It said, "You can migrate for 10 pounds!"

That did it! I took the train up to London from Ipswich and went along to Australia House in the Strand. I had to fill out all sorts of forms, have a medical and hand in my British passport. The deal was that if you stayed for two years in Australia, you could get your passport back and the trip to the antipodes would cost just ten pounds – if you returned within two years, you would have to pay back the full fare which was a lot of money in those days. You could choose whether to go by air or by sea. I choose to go by sea. I was given a 'Document of Identity' in lieu of my passport and was given a departure date for early May.

It was so easy. I really had no qualifications but I was young – I was 20 – and enthusiastic.

I rushed home and began to work long hours in the factory to save up some cash.

Deirdre and Charles were happy for me to go alone, not suspecting that I would stay here.

My plan was to give it a couple of years, then make my way back to the UK through India and the Middle-East. I was developing an interest in Eastern religion and philosophy and hoped to stay in an ashram in India and learn to meditate.

The cruise ship I was allocated was called the *Australis*, a Greek Chandros liner of 45,000 tons – quite big. My parents, Uncle Alan and Aunty Jacko and Uncle Bill came to see me off at Southampton. We had a few pints of beer in a local pub and then it was time to walk up the gangplank to get on board, after hugs all round. I was dying for a pee! I wet my pants a bit and what a relief it was to find a dunny on board. My cabin was on "F" Deck, below the waterline and not far from the engines. It had six berths, five of us were young Poms, and the sixth an Aussie heading home after his mandatory stint in Earl's Court, London.

Back up on deck, I waved to my family as we pulled away from the wharf, and like thousands of migrants worldwide, had a tear in my eye as I didn't know when I'd see them again. Fog soon enveloped the ship and the mournful bass note of the foghorn made me even more miserable.

Feeling sad didn't last long.

Australis – the liner that brought me to Australia in 1966

Every night on the ship there was a dance with a band, and it was a great opportunity to meet other passengers. We sailed over the Channel to Rotterdam and picked up some European migrants, then sailed down to the Med, stopping at Piraeus, the port for Athens in Greece. We had a laugh there – ending up in a tavern drinking cheap wine. I climbed up on a table, yelling out, "Vive le Greeks, Vive le Brits, Vive le Aussies!" then collapsing into someone's arms. We just managed to get back to the ship before she sailed. The other two ports of call were Port Said in Egypt and Aden in Yemen.

It was a British Protectorate back then in 1966. Poms were buying up lots of duty free stuff like record players, cameras and so on, not realising they would have to pay duty when we arrived in Australia. This caused a lot of angst and dismay among the passengers and was not a good start to their new country when they arrived.

Anyway, we finally fetched Fremantle after three and a half weeks. The *Australis* anchored offshore in Gage Roads on 1st of June and we headed for the rail to see what was happening. Immigration and the health department came on board and we were all lined up to check our paperwork and to be physically checked. A doctor looked down our throats, up our noses and into our ears! All the while, we were all making 'mooing' noises like cattle! It was hilarious but didn't impress the authorities.

We were finally allowed to enter Fremantle and step ashore in our new country. It was a Sunday and nearly everything was closed in those days. I shared a taxi with some of my fellow migrants and we were driven around Perth. I recall being impressed with the view from King's Park; the lovely Swan River and city skyline.

"Can we get something to eat?" we asked the cabbie. He took us to a café and on the menu were steak and chips or egg and chips, that was it. How Perth has changed, we are now multicultural and cosmopolitan and restaurants abound with food from all over the world. No al-fresco dining back then either: it was against health department regulations.

Next we asked the cabbie to take us to a pub so we could get a beer. Nothing much was open but he dropped us off in Hay Street and pointed to a doorway. "Go down there."

Well, the bastard stitched us up as it was a gay bar – blokes had green, red, orange and purple streaks in their hair!

So that was my introduction to Australia. We all laughed like hell and could see the funny side but we did wonder what we'd let ourselves in for – where was the bronzed Aussie in all those propaganda ads at Australia House in London?

Some passengers disembarked in Freo and more again in Melbourne. I saw my first Aussie Rules game of footy in a park somewhere in Melbourne and scratched my head as I couldn't understand the game at all. I eventually disembarked in Sydney and loved it.

Yes, I fell in love with Australia and was never homesick. In fact, I didn't return to England until nineteen years later. I loved the easy going feel of the place and enjoyed the humour. If you gave a bit of stick back when the Aussies called you a Pom or Pommie Bastard, they loved it!

Anyway, after a bit of time in Sydney, I was almost out of money so I used a free travel voucher to get to Brisbane on the train, where I began my working experiences, as mentioned previously.

The train had lots of young soldiers on board and I questioned them about what was happening. They told me they were going to basic training, then probably to Vietnam. They told me about the conscription ballot - every young bloke aged twenty went into the ballot and if your name was drawn out, you had to do national service, or 'nashos' as they called it. Bloody hell – no-one told me that at Australia House – I could have been picked and gone off to Vietnam.

Interestingly, some of my fellow migrants did get picked for "nashos." However, three of my cabin mates got very homesick and went back to the UK within three months. The attrition rate for migrants was high – no wonder the Aussies teased us, calling us, "To and Froms!" The problem when doing that was that they were not at home with the old UK life anymore either, then they would come back out here, still feeling in no-man's land.

Migrating to Australia now is much more difficult and costs a lot of money. I doubt they would take unskilled people like me either now but in those days, it was really up to you to make the best of it and enjoy the country. It was no use comparing it with life back in England, that just made some migrants unhappy. We speak the same language but there the similarity ends – Australia has its own identity and is not 'England in the Southern Hemishpere.'

I still love England and enjoy my visits and my Aussie second wife is somewhat of an Anglophile and loves it too – but we would not swap countries. Like all migrants from wherever, there will always be a little bit of England in me and a bit of their countries in them. And, really, hasn't that made for a more interesting place to live? Our cultural diversity is the envy of the world.

*****

In the months before I boarded the *Australis*, a young Swedish exchange student came to the village – as I mentioned at the beginning of this story. I was smitten by her and we got on well, not really into a heavy relationship but good friends. Margarita was her name and she was quite tall, a brunette with a shapely figure. I wanted the romance to develop. Anyway, after her stint in England was over, she went back to Sweden but invited me to stay with her family if I ever came to Sweden.

Well, the fishing was over and I was only working in the factory as a casual so I thought," Why not?"

So I bought a ticket for the ferry to Holland, an overnighter from Harwich. We arrived early in the morning at the Hook of Holland and I searched for the train station. My intention was to hide in the toilet until the train left the station, then grab a seat. If the ticket inspector came along, I'd get up and move. Anyway, I saw the mail carriage was open with lots of mail bags in it. I looked around and climbed on board, hiding amongst the sacks of mail. When the train reached Germany, I snuck off – I'd got away with it. From there, I hitch-hiked up through the north of Germany into Denmark and up the coast until I reached Williamshaven. To get the ferry to Gothenberg in Sweden was not expensive so I did buy a ticket. What a trip that was! The Swedes and Danes on board got absolutely plastered with the duty-free drinks – they were just chucking them back. A bloke explained that this was a regular fun thing to do of an evening. I joined in and had a few so it was a stilted walk off the ship and into the city as my knees were still not 100% after the crash.

I loved Gothenberg as it has lots of history and wonderful buildings. It was here I think I did one of the most stupid things I'd ever done, which I described at the beginning of the story.

A bus took me near Margarita's house and I made my way up a hill until I found her number and knocked on the door. It was about seven in the evening and beginning to get darker. Her dad opened the door and I asked, "Is Margarita in?"

He was gobsmacked – who was this English bloke?

Anyway, I was invited in. Margarita was as surprised as her dad.

Then began a wonderful two weeks. Margarita actually had a Swedish boyfriend but that didn't matter. I shared a room with her brother who was a nice bloke and we got on well. The dense pine forest was just at the back of their home and I was taken hunting for deer (they get to pest numbers and need culling). It was fantastic hacking our way through the undergrowth, trying to be quiet. The boys took a few shots but didn't hit anything. On another day, we spent time at a beautiful lake with some of Margarita's friends and they even had a swim but it was too bloody cold for me. The Swedes were most hospitable and I was made very welcome. Of course, it was a disappointment that she had a boyfriend but *thems the breaks*, as they say.

To get back to England, I had to borrow a bit of cash from the British Consul in Stockholm that I eventually paid back. So I was a legitimate passenger on the train and ferry for the return trip. I shudder now to think if I'd slipped off those bumpers and landed on the tracks to be squashed by the wheels – I was an idiot. I loved Stockholm too, especially the old part of the city with its cobbled stones and narrow streets.

As I entered Belgium on the way home, I began hitch-hiking again. An old Kombi van picked me up and I met a very interesting character, a Flemish guy called Walter de Buck. He turned out to be a sculptor and artist. When he found out how little cash I had, he invited me to stay at his place with his wife and other artists. I could help him in his studio to pay for my board and lodging.

Quite extraordinary, but it was a genuine offer and I worked hard in his studio helping sand down mock-ups of an air-conditioning tower he'd designed for a new building in Brussels. He seemed to work on many projects at the same time and other budding young sculptors were working with him too. After work, it was always off to a bohemian café in Ghent (where he lived) to drink beer and talk philosophy. I really loved it and had many hours of deep and meaningful conversation.

Walter was into eastern religion at that time and one afternoon we drove to a place and I met an Indian Guru. He was your stereotypical guru – long white beard and hair, flowing robes and he had a real twinkle in his eye. We sat at his feet and he explained that he was trying to synthesise eastern and western philosophy into a whole new understanding. All a bit beyond me but he seemed to be a very happy man – giggling now and then.

He turned to me and asked, "Are you searching?"

I replied, "Yes!"

And he said, "That's good – keep searching!"

I had hoped for a pearl of wisdom to get me through life!

Anyway, it made me think and I got stuck into the Upanishads and the Bhagavad Gita again – Hindu scriptures I'd begun reading and loved and carried around in my backpack.

It was a very pleasant and relaxed few weeks and I returned to England with a new interest and resolved to one day attend the Guru's ashram in India to learn more. It was not long after this that I applied to migrate to Australia, the intention being to stay my two years then head to India. That didn't happen. I fell in love with a beautiful Australian girl and we were married within six months.

Chapter Eight

Marriage and Children

"Trust that an ending is followed by a beginning"
Anon

This is a most difficult subject to write about. All marriages begin with such hope and enthusiasm and love. I had only been in Australia about seven months when we met. There I was in Perth after the hitch-hike across the Nullabor, doing odd jobs here and there to keep me going. I read about a free lecture on *The Origins of Evil* by a Theosophist called Stanley Spencer. Theosophy was a big organisation back in the 19th Century, founded by an eccentric lady called Madame Blavatsky. It took off all around the world and a branch was set-up in Perth. I don't remember anything about the lecture but I was drawn to this lovely young lady and could not take my eyes off her. She was eighteen and I was twenty-one and we fell madly in love almost immediately. Her name was Annette and she was gorgeous – beautiful figure, a lovely face, lots of wit and laughter and we got on so well. I guess you'd call it a whirlwind romance as we were married within six months. The proposal was rather weird – I mentioned that I wanted to go to India; she said I could go, so I countered with, "Let's get married!"

Annette was into all sorts of interesting stuff like astrology, palmistry, the occult, Tarot readings and so on. Being a sceptic myself, we did have some heated discussions about it all but mostly in fun.

We were married on July 2nd 1967 and were very happy together. Our first daughter, Samantha, was born on 23rd January 1969, about eighteen months later. Only thirteen months after, a second daughter, Carita, arrived on 3rd March 1970.

Both were beautiful, intelligent girls and we had lots of fun watching them grow up.

Samantha and Carita

To my permanent regret, after I got back into music, I began to play up. I was not a good faithful husband and I'm ashamed now by my lack of responsibility. Let's face it, I was a rotten bastard.

Home was always rented for the first years. We started by living on an orchard near Armadale: me doing some labouring, picking and sorting fruit for the markets, driving the tractor and generally having fun. It was easy after the 'roof plumbing' experience. The best crop was kiwi fruit — these had to be wrapped in tissue and placed carefully in a cardboard tray before being sent off to market. Oranges, lemons, mandarins, apples and grapes were also grown. We lived on the orchard with Annette's mum (she had recently left her alcoholic husband) and her brother Jim. One of the jobs we had to do weekly was empty the 'gas can' from the outside dunny. By the end of a week, it was pretty putrid and the only way Jim and I could handle it was to suspend it on a long pole as we carried it to its burial site! No showers — baths were in an old tin tub, the water heated in a big copper with a fire beneath, then it was bucketed into the tub. I always seemed to be last in the queue — mother-in-law first, then Annette, Jim, then me, reinforcing the old myth about Poms and bathing!

That adventure only lasted a while. After our wedding, held at a Theosophist's house in Floreat, we moved into a flat in Victoria Park. Annette was working for the State Library in the city and I was working for the Department of Agriculture by now, wool sorting and classifying. Nice clean work. When that contract ran out, I was offered that deildrin spraying job to control argentine ants. Dieldrin is a highly toxic chemical used to control insect pests, nasty stuff and is banned now.

It was a very happy time for us and it really only went pear-shaped when I took the drumming job up in Port Hedland, leaving my wife and young family. They joined me after a month or so and we even lived in the 'Nard Hotel until we sorted accommodation by buying a caravan. We then lived in it near the Walkabout Hotel. But the damage had been done and trust was broken as one of the barmaids told Annette that I'd been playing up.

Once we began performing at the Hedland Motor Hotel and the *Purple Haze* band was formed with Tony Tyler, we were offered a transportable home to live in round the back of the hotel. We rented out the caravan. Life went on and Annette forgave me but I'd still not learnt my lesson. When *Purple Haze* went touring and we were resident band at the Walkabout Hotels in Geraldton and Karratha, I began to stray again. Annette eventually took the girls and herself back to Perth. We were separated. I was young, stupid and selfish.

Samantha playing on the beach at Port Heldland

Whilst in Perth, about 1973, she became involved with a group called Divine Light Mission. This was an Indian organisation founded by a young Guru Maharaj Ji – handed the reins from his father. Maharaj Ji was very young when he proclaimed that he was going to bring peace to the world (after his father died). To do this, he moved to America and Divine Light Mission was established, soon spreading all over the western world, including Australia. To participate, you listened to Satsang – talks about life, spirituality and so on. Once you felt you were ready, a Knowledge session was set up with a swarmi (one of Maharaj Ji's close disciples) and you were taught the four techniques of mediation. These were light, sound, taste and breath and if you could concentrate well enough, there was a profound feeling of peace. It did feel a bit like a cult but there was never any pressure to stay or to hand over money. Annette told me about it and after quite a bit of Satsang, I was given the Knowledge techniques too. By this time, we were back together again and I'd settled down a bit.

Maharaj Ji, at that time, was looked upon as a manifestation of God. He was so young and yet these amazing insights were coming out of his mouth and it was always enthralling to listen to him. We even went to a couple of international festivals in the States and mixed with thousands of Premies (Premie literally means 'lover of God' in Hindu) from all over the world. It was a wonderful time – everyone was experiencing peace; there was no fighting and arguing even though queuing up for food and ablutions was a slow hassle. The main purpose of these huge events (a bit like Woodstock for music) was to be in Maharaj Ji's presence, and listen to him give Satsang and even to physically touch him – this is known as Dahshan, quite an uplifting experience.

I could never quite still my mind, stop all that useless chatter in one's head, so it was a bit difficult for me to meditate successfully for long periods – we were encouraged to try it for at least a half hour to an hour morning and night. To understand what I mean – try to become aware of your head chatting to you all the time, giving a constant commentary on life while you're awake; the goal of meditation is to experience the life force 'behind' thought – the energy that allows you to think.

I guess this was a fairly settled time for our marriage. For seven years we practised knowledge and went to the local meetings. The girls went to Claremont Demonstration School, the nearby primary. It was an excellent school. Both girls received a really good basic education and they both loved the school. Samantha was always more academic than Carita and topped her classes, but Carita was very creative and clever in her own way. We were all vegetarians during this period of our lives as that was also part of being a good Premie.

Divine Light Mission gradually folded during the mid-seventies but Marharj Ji kept going and the name changed to Elan Vital. I think that Maharaj Ji and his inner circle were afraid it would be classified as a religious cult so they shied away from publicity. These days he has gone back to his birth name, Prem Rawlat, and he is still teaching people how to meditate to gain inner peace. I guess you could say that he has brought peace to the world – not en masse but as an individual experience. He ran a series of TV shows called, "Words of Peace," on SBS. It's worth a look to see what it's all about.

*****

I did my teacher training at Graylands Teachers' College during that seven years as well. A steady income as a teacher enabled us to buy our first home after many years of renting. The tragedy is that the 'glue' that kept us together (DLM) was losing its grip on me and we began to drift apart again. I was brought up to be very tidy and organised – I guess because of my boarding school days where we had to make our own beds, keep our clothes lockers in order and be on time for everything. Annette and her family lived in relative chaos and I couldn't stand it. The worst bit was coming home from work and having to tidy up the house before I could relax. We still loved each other but the practicalities of daily life overwhelmed us and we eventually separated again.

Annette remarried and went on to earn a degree in psychology so she could help other women as a social worker.

She was always a strong person.

It was hard on the girls – Samantha was fourteen and Carita was thirteen. I feel horrible about it now and I guess I should have stayed until they left school. Carita went through a really bad patch and needed counselling and psychiatric help – even spending some months in an institution where we suspected the leading psychiatrist of sexually abusing her. Carita didn't say anything to me but confided in her sister. Carita never really went back to high school seriously and round about sixteen she'd had enough and headed off to Sydney with a girlfriend.

There, she did all sorts of casual jobs such as waitressing and so on, as well as some modelling. She began to take an interest in acting, taking lessons and producing some screen tests (which we've still kept). Her dream was to get into NIDA and she was working towards getting a scholarship when the girlfriend suggested she work in Japan as a hostess in a club. Many Aussie girls (as well as English, American, Kiwi and Canadian girls) did this apparently. It was good money for easy work. All the girls had to do was sit and talk to businessmen after work, encourage them to drink and make them feel 'special.' Japanese men loved western girls and Carita was very popular, being beautiful, intelligent and charming. By this time she had begun a relationship with an English guy called Robert, also a student who was studying law. They shared an apartment in Sydney and were very happy. It must have been really nice for Carita to have some stability back in her life. They even had a cat, Sinbad. When she was in Japan, Robert drew cartoons of him for her to ward off homesickness.

Samantha joined her sister in Sydney and they both travelled to Japan again for a third round of earning good money – Carita doing hostessing, Sam teaching English in a foreign language school.

Carita takes a break from modelling in Sydney

I have some wonderful letters from them – they found life very easy in Japan and they were both very popular. They shared a *gaigin* house with other Westerners who were all doing similar work. All the girls (and boys) felt that Tokyo was very safe – even though they were occasionally groped on the crowded trains. Samantha wrote, "We just yell at them and they slink off very embarrassed! … the loss of face being enough to deter any further advances."

So I think Annette and myself felt quite happy about them doing these tours to Japan. They were both earning far more money than any casual job in Sydney.

That was all due to change.

Chapter Nine

Losing a Child

"The hardest part of losing a child is living everyday afterwards."   Anon

I don't know how to write about this. It's something you never really recover from and a part of your heart dies forever. Counselling may help a bit but twenty-eight years later that hole has never been filled. The guilt I feel from leaving home when the girls were in their early teens has never gone away. It's something you have to live with – it's deep inside; you cannot really talk about it even with those you love. People do feel very uncomfortable talking to you about it. Writing about it is hard too – the keys feel like lead. I also think my ability to empathise and sympathise with others has been stunted a bit as well.

What happened to Carita?

Carita was into her third tour in Tokyo, working at a Ginza night club called *Ayakoji;* Sam was at her language school. One of the 'duties' of a hostess was to try and lure the businessmen into a *dohan* or date outside working hours where the girl might be offered presents, money or jewellery for spending a day with a customer. The *mama san* – the lady running the bar – would take a hefty cut of the fee and the girls would get extra bonuses if the customer was happy.

It's all very strange to us and we, naturally, think of it as a front for prostitution but, though that may have occurred,

Carita was not into that. She was earning plenty of money.

Tragically, her *dohan* date was with a Japanese/Korean man called Joji Obara, an extemely wealthy playboy who could be very charming and attentive. He was a regular at the *Ayakoji Club* and became familiar with all the hostesses, lavishing attention and presents on Carita in particular. He was your typical loner with no friends and lived in a fantasy world.

Once he had gained her confidence, the offer of the *dohan* date came up. *Mama san* approved it.

Robert, back in Sydney, was acutely worried as the date was going to extend into a weekend. Sam was worried too but Carita assured them both that Obara was harmless and just good company (he could speak good English).

*****

I was at school when I received a call from Sam saying, "Carita is very ill. You must come to Tokyo immediately. We don't know what it is – maybe some sort of hepatitis."

I booked a flight and was there within twenty-four hours. Sam met me at Narita Airport and we trained straight to the local Hideshima hospital close to their *gaigin* house. The night before I left for the airport, I had a vivid dream. Carita came to me; she was surrounded by light and then gradually faded into that golden light. I woke up crying and said to my wife, Aileen, "Carita has gone; she's died." I wrote that down and have kept it – it was so vivid. Beautiful, peaceful light but incredibly sad.

At Hideshima Hospital, Carita looked dreadful. Her skin had a yellowish tinge and she was on life support, unconscious. I sat with her for hours, talking about the things we'd done together in her childhood. Sam was really, really upset as she felt she'd let her sister down. From what Sam could deduce before Carita lost consciousness was that Obaba (he used an alias, "Nishida", for this *dohan*) had given her a spiked drink at his expensive apartment in the seaside suburb of Aburatsubo. Carita had felt something was wrong and tried to call Sam but Sam was busy. She was with her Japanese boyfriend Hidecki for the weekend and not at the *gaigin* house.

"Nishida" dropped Carita off at the local hospital on Monday morning claiming that she had food poisoning. She was still conscious at this stage but very groggy. The hospital got in touch with Sam and she rushed there not long before her sister lost consciousness. Carita couldn't tell her much.

Annette, Robert and I arrived to find Carita on life support and unconscious. They tried all sorts of tests and blood transfusions but no response. I think the hospital staff and doctors were very embarrassed by it and the next day she was rushed off to the huge Tokyo Women's Hospital by ambulance. We had to make our own way there by bus. A brain specialist was supervising treatment. They were giving her dose after dose of plasma transfusions and all sorts of tests. In the end the Doctor said, "She's brain dead – no responses at all." His diagnosis was that it was a very rare and deadly form of hepatitis (maybe E).

Sam and Robert wanted to keep the treatment going but Annette and I said that we had to let her go. We came back the next day and all the machinery and tubes surrounding her bed were turned off. Carita's breath slowly subsided and she left us. Robert and Sam were a mess. Annette and myself had to hold it together – it was bloody awful. Carita was wheeled out of ICU, then about an hour later, she was wheeled back in. Nurses had washed her hair, put on makeup and dressed her in a beautiful pink kimono. The whole bed was covered in flowers. Doctors and nurses all came to pay their respects, some crying, some with tears in their eyes, so apologetic that they hadn't been able to save her. It was all done in silence, very respectfully. I suppose how I was able to keep somewhat calm through it all was because of the dream and my belief that Carita had already left her body. Something I've never spoken about before is that I had this very real impression of Carita rolling up and down her own physical body (in spirit form) saying, "It's ok, dad, it's ok, dad."

Carita was taken down to the basement of the hospital and put in a Buddhist shrine. She was placed on a raised dais with lots of flowers around, tinkling bells and incense. We stayed with her for the night.

What came next was a horrible shock.

At some stage, we were called into an office somewhere in the basement and quite rudely asked for $250,000 (a quarter of a million dollars) for her treatment. Annette and I were desperate: we didn't have that sort of money. Sam brought Hidecki in to interpret – telling the authorities we couldn't pay.

It was horrible after all the respect from the medical staff. The admin 'suits' were not sympathetic at all. Anyway, after investigation, it was found that Samantha had taken out insurance for foreign workers with her language school and she had put Carita on the policy too. The bill was paid.

The next part of it all was organising a cremation in Tokyo. Again, Hidecki was able to help with this and it was all arranged. In Japan, funerals and cremations are quite different. You can bypass the next part if you'd rather not know.

The coffin – when the funeral directors arrived we had to pick Carita up (in Japan, the father takes the top half of the body, the mother the lower half). Rigor mortis had set in and Carita was very light so it was not difficult. We placed her gently in the casket then the whole casket was filled up with flowers before the top went on. All employees involved wore white gloves, dark suits, white shirts and black ties. Each one had to be given a 'tip' in a plain envelope. It was all done in silence with much bowing.

Annette and I were driven to the crematorium in the hearse. There, Japanese families had gathered to say goodbye to their loved ones. The ovens were all open, with roaring fires inside. The casket is placed on rollers, the lid comes off and we could kiss Carita goodbye before she went into the flames. We were then ushered into a waiting room as the casket was pushed into the oven. It sounds macabre but it wasn't. After a bit of time, we were asked to go back in. Carita's bones and ashes were brought out and we were given metal chopsticks to pick out the largest pieces and place them into an urn along with her ashes – the top of her skull on top. It sounds awful to our western ears but it was very moving and another chance to say goodbye right at the very end.

We carried her remains onto the plane in a fairly large urn for the flight home to Perth. We had another 'normal' service for family and friends back here. She died on 29th February, 1992, just three days before her 22nd birthday. We laid her to rest at Karrakatta. What a waste of a beautiful person. Not a day goes by when I don't think of her and what she might have done with her life.

*****

This is not the end of this story. Even more bizarrely, we actually met "Nishida" in Tokyo. How the hell did that happen? Annette and I had accepted that Carita's death was accidental, perhaps food poisoning or picking up the hepatitis bug but both Sam and Robert were suspicious. Sam tried to get the Tokyo police involved but they weren't interested, nor was the Australian Embassy. They were polite and sympathetic but thought that it would be impossible to mount an investigation.

Samantha received a call from "Nishida" saying he wanted to meet Carita's parents. It was arranged that we'd meet (after the cremation) at a hotel (I can't recall the name) and were given a room number. Sam and Hideki came with us but Nishida refused to see them. Annette and I were ushered into a hotel suite by a well-dressed young man. He was sweating profusely. He had a very limp handshake. We took seats and he gave us a drink and offered us some snacks. He then proceeded to break into tears, saying how much he loved Carita and was so sorry about her death. He reckoned he was Carita's boyfriend and was going to propose to her. He appeared very visibly upset – that's all I can remember now, except that he offered Annette some expensive jewellery. He said he'd bought it for Carita's birthday and wanted us to have it. The meeting didn't last long.

He just kept blubbering and saying how sorry he was. I thought he was sincere but Annette was very uneasy about his story of the food poisoning (supposedly oysters).

One unusual thing I do recall was that as we left the room and walked down the corridor, he stuck his head out of the door to watch us go. He had a strange look on his face.

Sam and Hideki had tried to get the police to come along but to no avail. It was years later that we discovered that the "Nishida" we'd met was actually Joji Obara himself. It makes us both feel sick in the stomach to know we came face to face with our daughter's killer.

Chapter Ten

Obara's Arrest, Trial and Sentencing

Aileen and I were up in Darwin in 2001, staying on our yacht at a marina when I received a call from Sam. She said, "Carita was killed – she didn't die of food poisoning."

It was a huge shock, a bolt out of the blue. Apparently, Robert (by now a practising lawyer) had looked into the case of Lucie Blackman and felt that the man accused of her murder and disappearance, Joji Obara, may have had something to do with Carita's death. He flew to Tokyo and badgered the police and got them to investigate. (It is difficult for us to appreciate how slow the authorities work in Japan). Tony Blair, the British PM at the time, had talks with the Japanese PM and that pushed the investigations along.

Eventually, it was found that Obara had raped and videoed about 400 girls, both Western and Japanese. The Lucie Blackman case was sensational world-wide and I won't dwell on it here. Suffice to say, there was enough evidence for Obara to be arrested. Annette flew to Tokyo to identify Carita who was one of the girls Obara had videoed performing his horrible fetish, wearing a 'Zorro' mask.

It was absolutely traumatic for her and the nightmare has stayed with her.

Part of his ritual was to serve the girls a spiked drink, then to render them unconscious with chloroform. While unconscious, he performed his sexual perversions (all on video). Very weirdly, he kept records of his *conquests*, making notes about the girls, who were both Western and Japanese. He called it 'play.' Next to Carita's entry, he'd written, *"Too much chloroform"*.

It was part of the evidence that helped convict him. The other crucial piece of evidence was a liver sample the doctor at the Tokyo Women's Hospital had kept. The liver biopsy showed a massive dose of chloroform had killed her liver. By some miracle, the hospital had kept that small biopsy sample for ten years. Why we weren't informed at the time is a mystery. I think the Japanese just wanted us out of the country as soon as possible – the 'saving face' syndrome.

The trial began on 4th July 2001 and ran for six years until April 24th 2007. A huge bulk of evidence had to be sifted through. I had recorded calls with the Tokyo police many times and we all wrote impact statements. It was an agonising process, we all had to be patient. We all flew up to Tokyo, including Aileen, for the final verdict – the courtroom was packed and hundreds of journalists and cameras were outside and inside. We held a very moving press conference with lots of Japanese reporters just staring at us. It had been the most horrible crime in Japan in recent times.

Judge Tochigi – it was a panel of three judges, no jury – droned on and on. The Blackman's were there too – all of us expecting guilty verdicts for Lucie and Carita. It was silent until he said Obara was not guilty of Lucie's death. Reporters ran out of the court to contact their respective medias.

Then he said that Obara was guilty of raping and killing Carita. Uproar!

Obara had sat through six years of evidence, showing no remorse and denying it all. He was not far away, in front of us and showed no emotion at the guilty verdict.

*****

In 2008 he made an appeal. I flew up to Tokyo twice to negotiate with his lawyers (he had a lot). They tried to get me to sign 'statements' to say that Carita had died from food poisoning after eating bad oysters. I refused but did agree to say that maybe he could be rehabilitated sometime in the future. I believe that anyone can be rehabilitated if they have the will. It was intimidating being grilled in my hotel room – but I used the room phone to keep in touch with Samantha, Annette and Aileen. The upshot of it all was that he offered us compensation money – not uncommon in Japan – and that was supposed to show his remorse and maybe help lessen his life sentence. The judge dismissed it and his life sentence stands. He's still in prison now.

How do I feel about him now? I can't forget his horrible crimes but I think I have tried to forgive him. Annette, Sam and Robert still hate him. I don't think he deliberately set out to murder Carita but he did murder Lucie Blackman in the most grotesque way and attempted to cover it up. He was eventually convicted of her murder too.

Chapter Eleven

Happier Times

"If the second marriage succeeds, the first one didn't really fail"   Mignon McLaughlin

One afternoon in 1983, I took myself along to the old Railway Hotel in North Fremantle to listen to some jazz with the *Cornerhouse Jazzband*. Our jazzband, the *Storyville Jazzband*, had recently filled in for CH at the Railway while they took a break and I was curious to check it out as an audience member. It was an afternoon that changed my life. I met my second wife, Aileen, there. We were both separated at the time. I saw her in a red dress and she was 'writhing' against the wall in time to the rhythm of the band! She denies this, of course. I just had to speak to her and when the band took a fifteen minute break, we chatted. I must admit I was bloody scruffy: I only had on a pair of tatty, old, cut-off denim shorts, and an ordinary shirt. Anyway, we seemed to hit if off immediately and we made a date to see each other. Thirty-seven years later we are still together. We married after seven years 'living in sin' on 26th January 1991, (Australia day) – how could I ever forget that anniversary?

My lovely wife, Aileen

Aileen was very different – my first marriage to Annette was always under a bit of tension as it's very hard for the tidy to live with the untidy (or the opposite). Aileen was so organised and her home was immaculate, nothing to clean up and I felt at ease. We both loved jazz and travel and we'd spend many hours just enjoying each other's company. It was love at first sight. Dixie, *Storyville's* bandleader, used to say he could see doves flying about when Aileen and I were together.

She is a fourth generation Aussie and very proud of her heritage. Her great-grandfather, Laurie Sinclair, was the bloke whose horse, *Norseman,* kicked over a bit of dirt and came across that huge gold nugget that caused a gold rush and the establishment of the town of Norseman. It's a fascinating story and you can read about it in the family history, *"In Search of Elizabeth,"* by Janice M. Young. Aileen also comes from gypsy stock and her branch of those famous wanderers settled in the Shetlands, to the north of Scotland. Quite unusual for gypsies, as they were not known for being seafarers. She claims her love of travel and adventure comes from the gypsies.

I was very keen to introduce her to the world of sailing but our first little voyage was almost a disaster. We left Perth Flying Squadron in my little 20-footer, *Sundance*, sailed up the Swan River and motored under the Fremantle traffic bridges. Once into the Indian Ocean, I set a course for Carnac Island. Aileen was very confused as we were not pointing at Carnac. After explaining the 'theory of tacking', I think she understood, and after some time we fetched the island. By this time she was dying for a pee. There was no head (toilet) on this little yacht so I offered to carry her ashore. She refused and held on until we sailed right back to PFSYC! It's a wonder she agreed to see me again but she could see the funny side (later!!).

It was not long before we were living together, though before that, I was sharing digs with friends after I'd moved out of our family home. I left the house to Annette and just said goodbye with a suitcase, towel and my drums.

It's never easy breaking up; lots of guilt is attached at first and you do wonder if you should have stayed for the 'sake of the kids.' But you can't beat yourself up forever – eventually life sorts us out anyway.

Aileen had gone out to Libya three years previously with her husband but one day they realised that they had nothing left of their relationship and split up. They had two grown up children, Greg and Suzanne. She had her own flat and job in Libya and it was one of the most liberating times of her life. After three years and missing family, she returned to Perth to live on her own. Her husband stayed on in Libya.

So we were both separated and not really looking for someone else, but fate steps in and what can you do?

She has been a marvellous wife, so supportive and a real home-lover. She's put up with the music and sailing for years. She even went to Fremantle TAFE night school with me to learn coastal navigation and pass her Radio Operators licence. We made a great team on our yachts as Aileen learnt to sail, take the helm and handle the vessels under power while I did all the deck work.

An old sailor at PFSYC, Frank Knox, used to encourage her, continually saying, "YOU TAKE THE HELM – let him do the work!"

We often had to remind other skippers about that and successfully got other girls to take the helm as well. There was nothing worse to us than seeing yachts (or power boats) come into an anchorage with the skipper yelling excited, angry instructions to his wife (or partner) on the foredeck trying to manhandle a heavy anchor. Stupid! But we've seen it over and over again. "Manhandle" is the right word – the male should handle the heavy deckwork.

Aileen is a good navigator too and it was always a joint decision to plot our day's sailing directions on the charts. To have two heads planning the waypoints for the day was good for safety as well.

One of the really worthwhile things we've done together was to kick off Cruising in Company after we moved over to Hillarys Yacht Club from the public marina. All us sailors who had yachts but didn't want to race just sort of pottered around in our own boats. We got everyone involved in cruising together and having much more fun. We would organise weekends away, radio skeds, sundowners on each other's boats and I even started some coastal navigation classes at the club. It's now an important section of the club and continues on.

During our many years together, Aileen has helped design the three homes we've had built. It's another of her passions and she loves planning the décor and layout of the rooms. I just go along with it. But not only that, we have lived 'small' too, as we've lived aboard yachts for over five years in total. Her favourite house was the one we built in Mandurah. This was in Mandurah Quay, a really lovely part of the city that is on the corner of Peel Inlet and the Estuary. We made many friends and loved the lifestyle, but one thing prevented us from living there permanently – family. We could not get the family to drive down to see us (maybe once or twice a year) and we eventually got fed up with driving back and forth to Perth. So we built our final home in Gwelup.

As for living small, if two people can live in the confined space of a yacht over long periods I guess it says a lot for their relationship. It's not easy but the fun we had sailing the oceans outweighed the difficulties and frustrations at times. On a yacht there is only one skipper but the 'admiral' has complete control of her side of the living arrangements – plus, in our case, shared responsibility for the navigation and radio communication. I love her dearly but do not express it often enough!

Another of Aileen's passions is gardening. My parents were both good gardeners but they never encouraged me to join them in the garden. Aileen is one of those people with a green thumb and always has a garden established in our homes. I am just the labourer. I never knew the difference between a daffodil and a daisy! I always think of gardening as, "Dirty, Dangerous, Expensive and Smelly!" and have never understood the pleasure it gives. But there you are, each to their own.

It's not all roses though, as we are both pretty strong-minded with definite views on things so we do have heated arguments at times. But overall, we've got a very good marriage. She is a very loyal person and has retained close relationships with our sailing friends and her book club. Cooking is another great skill of hers. I love to get into the kitchen as well but as I'm inclined to make a bit of a mess, Aileen prefers to cook most meals.

She worked at PMH for thirteen years as the PA for the head of ICU at the hospital. It was a demanding role as she often had to deal with distraught parents and a demanding boss. She handled it all well with calm and efficiency. The only time she was reprimanded was when she took a morning off to see me arrive back home on *Lotus 11* – her boss didn't quite realise what a big moment it was for us after seven weeks with no communication!

Aileen and me – a very happy couple

Aileen's family have accepted me and we get on well, except for her son, Greg, who is a bit of a loner and is estranged from the family. Suzanne is lovely, a great 'greenie' and passionate conservationist. She is also a talented kindy teacher at a well-known Perth girl's school – the staff, parents and little kids love her. We often tease her about the 'Grass Shakes' she makes for breakfast – lots of green stuff like kale, celery, spinach and so on! It looks and smells awful but she says it does her good. Suzanne and her husband Clive are very adventurous climbers and trekkers and have conquered many challenging climbs, even getting to Base Camp at Everest.

My own daughter, Samantha, married an American and they lived in New York up until the 9/11 attacks on the Twin Towers. They rented an apartment not far away and experienced the awful aftermath. Their first child, 'T', was born in NY but they decided to move out of the city after that and bought a nice house in Pennsylvania. It was all going well and two more boys were born, 'B' and 'D'. The story gets tricky after that as Sam's husband lost his job in NY. He was teaching and helping install sound equipment for a college in the city. He says he caught someone embezzling funds and was sacked when he brought it before management.

Finding it hard to get work, they sold up everything and came to live in Perth. Life has been tough for them. Sam's husband has never really found his feet here and has only managed to obtain casual work. The really sad thing is that we have drifted apart. I don't think it's my fault as we're always encouraging her family to join us for picnics and stuff, as they have no extended family here. 'R' is a very talented person but inclined to get into conspiracy theories about people out to get him and blocking his attempts to get ahead in Oz. I try to keep an open mind but am sceptical – I really don't like blame as a way of life and am not into victim playing.

Samantha has always been gifted academically. She won a scholarship to Churchlands Senior High as a music student, her instruments being the clarinet and flute. I think she found the course pretty taxing, as she has not really played much since leaving school. She is well travelled and worked for United Airlines as a fight attendant, reaching the position of burser and getting into the training side. Back here in Perth, Sam gained an Honours in Science at ECU and now works there in the labs and assists foreign students.

Sam with her professor, Magda. A proud moment.

As a mum with three sons and a husband struggling to find work, she has been the rock of that family – incredibly hard working. My grandees are nice boys. 'T' has become an IT expert, 'B' a talented artist and musician, and we're waiting to see what 'D' gets into. They seem a happy, insular family so I guess I have to accept that.

It is difficult to watch Sam's family and Aileen's son drift away, as both Aileen and myself grew up in close-knit families where the extended family was important.

My parents, aunts, uncles, grandparents have all 'gone to

God' and there is only my brother and I left. He is a bit of a recluse now and doesn't seem interested in keeping in touch. Deirdre and Jacko both died from dementia, which is a bit of a worry. Anyone who has experienced dementia in their family will know what I mean – it's not very pleasant to watch near the end.

I'm very fortunate to have Aileen's family. They are great Aussies and I think they quite enjoy having an ex-Pom in the family. One thing I still support the Poms in is test cricket so you can imagine that we have a bit of family banter over that!

Chapter Twelve

Musings in The Time of Corona

"There are more things in heaven and earth, Horatio, than are dreamt of in your philosophy"
Shakespeare (Hamlet)

and

"He's got a good future behind him!"   Acker Bilk

Do we ever really retire? In my case, doing work for salaries and wages has been replaced by doing work as a volunteer and keeping very busy – sometimes too busy. Aileen is quite happy to potter around at home (Dixie dubbed her 'er indoors.' after Arthur's never seen wife in the BBC production, *Minder*. It's stuck and I call her that too.

After twenty-one years teaching primary school, when I retired I switched to high school and enjoyed another sixteen years relief teaching. My main areas were English and Humanities and Social Sciences, although I was prepared to do anything and that meant that I could find myself in any department – good fun.

Of course, the pay was handy and has enabled us to do lots of travelling; something we both love.

Now I'm into my 70s the phone has stopped ringing. Maybe a bit of ageism has crept in but I don't really mind, I have lots of other things to do. I have joined U3A (University of the Third

Age), do a few public talks, have become a Rottnest Island Guide and also a guide for visitors on the *Duyfken,* a lovely replica of the sailing ship that briefly explored 300 kilometres of Australia's coast on Cape York, in 1606. I keep my hand in on the drums with three jazz bands and with our rock 'n' roll band *Purple Haze*. We reformed in 2009 with three of its original members: Greg (Bazz) Clarke, Harry Allen and myself. We added a very fine guitarist, Robbie Jones, and almost immediately, bookings began to arrive. Sadly, Harry (Hazza) died at the early age of seventy-two with heart problems. His place was taken by Rod Christian, mentioned earlier in the story. A very fine bass player, composer and gifted music teacher, Rod has kept us honest in the harmony department, something I'm really enjoying. Rod has written some lovely compositions: his 60's musical, *Cruisin'* has been performed world wide and he has composed a tribute to his mum and dad's wartime experiences with another musical, *Mates*.

We are a fun unit, though we have very different temperaments and values but seem to fire well on stage. We have dropped the 'Purple' part of the name now and just call ourselves *The Haze Showband*.

The Haze Showband: Rod, Bazz, me and Robbie

We play all sorts of gigs and dances and, though there is not much money in it these days, it's bloody good fun. Our combined ages add up to something like 285 years and we've all played music since our teens, right through our careers in day jobs. We reckon if the '*Strolling Bones*' (Rolling Stones) can keep playing, so can we.

*****

With the end not so far off, have I learnt anything? Gathered up any wisdom? Well, I think we have all learnt a new way of life with the spread of COVID-19. As I write, the whole world is almost shutting down, borders are closing and we are all being encouraged to stay at home as much as we can. Having had it 'so good' (to quote 60s British PM Harold McMillan), we can't really complain if this thing gets us in our third age. As I wrote at the beginning, we have been the luckiest generation ever to inhabit Planet Earth. And ain't that the truth? So, if we lose a few of us in our old age, it's not too much of a disaster.

Some things I have learnt over the years are:

a) Don't show photos of your grandkids to folk (especially on your phone!)
b) Don't show people photos of your travels (especially on your bleedin' phone!)
c) Get used to becoming invisible as you get older. You gradually become irrelevant – to counteract this, I like to look at people when I'm out and about and often get a tiny smile or nod.
d) Aileen and I have travelled a lot and we agree that people are ok everywhere. Those really nasty bastards are only the tiniest cohort of humanity – but they get the biggest headlines, don't they? Folk are nice.
e) De-clutter! Leave this earth with very little stuff! (We've had to clean out two homes and it's not easy).

Is that a bit of wisdom?

The social isolation due to the virus had Aileen looking for jobs for me to do around the house. I am enjoying a bit of time to do more writing and reading. I realise that I had got myself into a very busy lifestyle with all the volunteering and the music – maybe too busy and not leaving much time for reflection. As Patrick Carlton wrote in his column in the *Herald Sun*, "Why rush back to normality?" It's a great article espousing a more relaxed way of life, concluding that some of us may not be ready, "to present ourselves to the world again. We may never be".

Another fascinating viewpoint I discovered on this dilemma was on ABC Radio National. The presenter was saying that for shy people, the lockdown and social distancing has been a blessing. Those of us who are a bit shy can retreat into our world of imagination and not have to worry about socialising, making 'small talk' and so on. The downside is that our 'social muscle,' which we've had to develop to deal with the world, may atrophy and it may be harder to get out there into the scrum of daily life again. We will have to start working on it and relating to folk again.

Its incredible how this pandemic brought us all closer together. Modern communications are so advanced that we can tune into TV programmes to see exactly what is happening in other parts of the world. Not to mention things like Face Time on phones, Facebook, Zoom, Instagram, Twitter (what's that?) emails and the internet as well – they all keep us in touch. So far, in WA, we have had it pretty easy. Our state government jumped on it quickly and reduced the spread of cases. We are not out of the woods yet but much better off than many countries.

Cruise ships will take a long time to recover from this. Lots of cases have come from the confines of cruise ships, many blaming the air-conditioning on board. I tend to think it's more to do with the close proximity of fellow passengers who are coughing or sneezing, the failure to use the hand-disinfectant and not washing hands enough. The bug can live for quite some time on hard surfaces and there's plenty of those on a ship.

I wonder if the community togetherness and support will continue after it's over? Our capitalist way of life with its consumer madness and over consumption has slowed right down. Our whole economic system and security is based on someone making products, growing products or digging up stuff – and us buying it – the 'supply and demand' principle – but that's gone out of the window for the moment. We have become almost socialistic. A right-wing government is handing out money to prop up small business and to us as consumers, hoping we'll go out and spend it to keep the wheels turning. Rents are being subsidised, loans put on hold. It's amazing. If we can look after our citizens in hard times like this – why can't we when things are booming? You have to question the whole system. And where is all this money coming from? What is the World Bank? What is the IMF (International Monetry Fund)? Where do *they* get all *their* money? It seems to me that no one needs to live in poverty, there are huge funds stockpiled and it just needs redistributing – this virus has proved that. The mega billionaires could spend some of their money helping to bail out the economies of their own countries – no need to cripple the poor taxpayer. I'm not against entrepreneurs and business, we need them but after they've made their millions they might find it more satisfying being philanthropic, as many do. A good example is Scott Farquhar, the multi-billionaire Aussie who's made his massive fortune from IT. He gives a lot of money to non-profit organisations that are assisting people in need. He is trying to get every company in the world to donate just 1% of their profits to eliminate poverty – a really great idea.

How many millions or billions does one person need? Sickness is the great leveller. Of course, the wealthy will get better treatment for any virus and have a better chance of recovery but it's still a thing that has affected all stratum of society. In America, it's the African Americans and latinos who are dying in the greatest numbers.

One lovely news story I heard was that a leading Perth hotel was taking in the homeless, offering them rooms, toiletries and food. The hotel manager said it was one of the most rewarding experiences he's ever had in his career. Isn't that wonderful?

If I were into conspiracy theories, I'd be thinking that this has been unleashed on the world by the Chinese. The whole world gets infected and then they supply the equipment to fix it – thus improving their own economy while putting the rest of us into debt. This economic takeover seems to be happening in third world countries anyway, as massive loans are given by China to improve the infrastructure of underdeveloped countries. They then have a huge debt to pay back, thus making them even more dependent on China. It remains to be seen if China is going to be a benevolent world power and perhaps take over as world leader after the Americans. With trade wars looming, it's not looking so good for the West.

Another interesting thought is what's happening in third world countries? They, obviously, cannot practice social isolation as so many people live together, jam packed into small homes in shanty towns and such. You'd think the virus would spread like mad through those societies yet we don't hear very much about the true numbers in the media. It may cause untold deaths like the Spanish 'flu of 1918.

Alternatively, here's a thought: did the Creator unleash the virus on us so that we learn to appreciate this planet? More conspiracy, of course, but we do need to reassess our lifestyle and take a look at our very self-indulgent lives. We can't just continue with the rich getting richer by the day and the masses, who live below the poverty line, struggling to survive. Do we really think that it's possible with our economic system that *everyone in every country* will be able to own a house, two cars, fridges, washing machines, dish washers, i-pads, mobile phones, desktop computers, eat out or live on take-away food?

But that seems to be the story: "Jobs and Growth" for all. It just can't happen, there are just too many people – but it's what advertising tells them they can have. Many future jobs will just involve people helping other people who'll never work and don't know what to do with their lives. The planet will suffocate under the stress of all our consumerism. And all that e-waste with products that have built-in obsolescence – where is that rubbish going to go?

Mental health seems to have become a big issue now. I wonder if it has anything to do with individualism as a way of life – rather than community?

"It's all about me, what I want, I've got my rights – so bugger off!" bleat some folk.

Living for material possessions, getting one up on others, or trying to be 'cool' and 'in' is bad for one's mental health.

If you created this Earth, would you really like to see it ruined and unliveable – no! You'd do something about it. If, as religions tell us, we are created in God's image and we do have a spark of divinity in us then we are not going to let it happen, are we? It is hard to believe there is not *evil* in the world but I tend to think of evil as stupidity, selfishness and greed.

Living close! How many couples must have struggled to be in each other's company 24/7? It's a big ask. We are so used to constant stimulation: going out, eating out, flying around the world, driving everywhere at high speed, meeting up with family and friends, jumping on cruise ships – to have to be cooped up with your one and only is a new social dynamic and I do worry about an escalation of domestic violence. I guess that as Aileen and I have lived small on yachts for five years (on and off) it may be easier for us – and my 51 days (seven weeks and two days) of solo sailing across the Southern Ocean *with no communications at all* has steeled me to not feel lonely. It was my own version of forty days and forty nights in the desert!

Going out to the shops or for a walk, it almost seemed that the whole community was breathing a big sigh of relief. We can slow down and still enjoy life. We have become human beings instead of 'human doings!' Just looking at our calendar with no meetings on it was scary at first but now I'm enjoying it (no gigs, no public talks, no Rotto guiding, no Duyfken, no U3A, no coffee / dinner dates).

Keeping our social distance actually brought us closer together. Going for a walk locally, people were all smiles and "hellos" and neighbours were looking after each other. We even had a note in our letterbox asking if we needed help with some shopping or any other jobs. And another neighbour dropped off a nice bottle of red at our front door, with a short note to say, "Thanks for being nice neighbours!"

Personally, I would be happy to sacrifice a bit of my third age to keep the economy going for the younger generations. It's heartbreaking to see those queues outside Centrelink. If younger people have lost work to keep us old farts from catching the virus, that's very selfless but are we really worth it? It's a real moral dilemma. Why weren't we asked if we should 'let it rip' (let the virus loose and knock off lots of us older generation) – then build up what's called 'herd immunity?' How many of us boomers would have said, "Ok guys, we've had a good time – now we don't want to hold you back or put you further into debt – so let CV19 rip and you have a good time too!"

What really worries me is the huge number of unemployed, uneducated men around the world who can't get work – you see them rioting on TV in many countries, but what can governments do? Someone is going to have to teach them to live fruitful lives without, possibly, ever going to work; or are we going to have to redefine what 'work' is?

Another worry is the way many younger people are relying on social media for their news and current events. Social media (just like this chapter) is more about opinion than hard facts. You can't believe it is gospel truth. The ABC and SBS probably bring us the most honest news in Australia.

*****

I have begun to rethink some philosophy. Any philosopher is difficult to read – try it. We all remember Descartes, "I think, therefore I am", but other philosophers are hardly ever mentioned now. It's become a rather bloodless academic subject with its own language that is quite obtuse.

It should be fun. We're all interested in the meaning of life, why we're here: is there a purpose for our existence? Some lovely quotes I can recall are:

"Leisure is the mother of philosophy" – (Hobbes) Isn't that true? Being busy keeps ideas at bay and gives little time for reflection.

And: *"Philosophy is just a by-product of misunderstanding language!"* (Wittgenstein) Brilliant quote – so why bother to study it?

Religions have tried to answer those big questions, of course, but to join in, you have to take a leap of faith and trust in the stories and dogma. I'm pretty sure the incredible men who trod the earth and were the initial focus of the main religions: Jesus, Mohammad, Buddha, Confucious, Moses, the authors of the Hindu Upanishads and Bhagavad Gita – did not envisage, or want, huge systems and organisations built from their teachings. They were all telling us to look inside ourselves to find truth and wisdom and that rites and rituals were not the goal of self-realisation. I dunno – not having achieved self-realisation, it's hard to comment. I just know that organised religion has caused far more harm to life on earth than benefits.

We are, as seniors, advised to keep up three things in our lives – some physical exercise, some brain activity and to socialise with others. I call it the three-legged stool – take one leg away and the stool topples over! So it's a good system to follow but where do the legs fit? They are glued into a *top or seat* and to me that seat is the most important bit and we could call it 'spiritual' – *not religious*. We all yearn for that inner peace, ecstasy and enlightenment and get glimpses of it in music, dance, poetry, sex, art and literature. Did COVID-19 give us a bit of breathing space to experience the *"Peace which passeth all understanding?"* that Paul spoke about? Rushing about being busy, I suspect, won't lead to inner peace.

Let's face it – travel had got out of hand. We were crawling all over planet earth like ants, burning up huge amounts of fossil fuels in cars, trains, aircraft and cruise ships. 16,000 aircraft were grounded around the world due to the downturn in travel and the almost 300 cruise ships sailed back to their home ports. What an incredible saving of fossil fuel.

An interesting side effect of us staying at home has been a big reduction of carbon, methane and monoxide in the atmosphere and that it is having a positive effect on climate change. Makes you wonder, doesn't it? Northern Indians can now see the Himalayas, Chinese cities are clear of smog, rivers are looking clean and the sky looks clearer. They even found jelly fish in the canals of Venice – usually very murky water. The most diehard, anti-human climate change skeptic would surely have to admit that mankind has had a negative effect on the environment now.

Even though we have been on five cruises and have really enjoyed the experience, always at the back of my mind is that it's a very decadent activity and a manifestation of Western over indulgence. All that food! It was horrifying to see some fellow passengers loading up their plates in the lido buffet on the top decks and going back for more and more. Maybe the buffet will be banned in future? I have been expecting a terrorist attack on a cruise ship as they are highly visible symbols of us Western infidels overdoing it.

The future? Let's hope we have one. I'm optimistic, as there are very many clever people out there who can point us in the right direction. But surely we do have to stop cutting down all the forests, causing animals to become extinct and clearing the oceans of sea life? It's a no-brainer. Blokes have been really clever inventing all this technical stuff but now it's our ladies who need to start running the economic, political, business and social side of life. I'm sure women could run the world better than men and leave the men to design and build more clever toys to save our environment (of course, women can do the technology bit as well as blokes, if they want).

I have always enjoyed women's company and really do think our western women could lead the world into much fairer societies. Women from third world countries would eventually follow as they gradually shake off the shackles of male domination.

Funny thing – I remember at high school we were allocated one main book for history. It was titled *Outlines of English History* and I can clearly recall saying to Rector Vincent (he took us for history). "But sir, this is just a list of kings, queens and wars!"

He replied, "Yes, Ridgway, you're right, but you need to remember the dates to pass your exams!"

And that's it – our history has been one of wars and inventing more and more efficient ways to kill each other. Let's give women a go – they will do a far better job of leading us into the future.

Enough of the too serious musings and let's think about humour. Humour is a fantastic way of poking fun at ourselves. Life is actually more Monty Pythonish than orderly and predicable and if we can have a bloody good laugh, it really helps. Remember the Reader's Digest, 'Laughter is the Best Medicine?' Being an ex-Pom, I'd have to say that I think British humour is the best, although we do have many great comedians in Oz now. I love Kitty Flanagan, Roy and HG and the irrepressible Kathy Lette and Sammy J.

Funny how none of the aforementioned great spiritual teachers ever used humour in their teachings, isn't it? I wonder why? Maybe they did – or did the fanatical followers who later wrote up what they said delete it? A message can often get through to us better with humour than by the old 'fire and brimstone' preaching! I wonder if and when the Messiah does come back – how will he (or she) handle the media? All TV stations will be clamouring for interviews, special in-depth discussions and so on – and what a media circus it would be. With the twenty-four hour news cycle, how would the Messiah go the next day or week?

As a silly old sod I reckon I can toss ideas around without having to justify them. I'd love to be able to experience Blake's insight and know that:

"*Everything that lives is holy, life delights in life.*"

and not end up pessimistic like T.S. Eliot who wrote:

"*I have measured out my life with coffee spoons*"

Or: "*Will the veiled sister pray for the children at the gate,*

who will not go away and cannot pray.?" (Eliot found his salvation in the Catholic Church).

Perhaps his most pessimistic lines were

"*Where is the life we lost in living?*" and "*Birth, copulation, death, that's all the facts when you get down to brass tacks.*"

Which is the essence of what all those spiritual men were

trying to tell us - as well as John Lennon who said,

"Life is what happens to you while you're making other plans."

That is very profound but it is not easy being in the 'now' experiencing mindfulness.

So I don't want to end up feeling like Eliot but have to admit that sometimes just being busy is a way to put off 'grand' thoughts – though when we are busy in creative endeavours, we do experience the 'now.' I think that's why live music and performance is so captivating for both muso and audience and why we want to keep on playing for as long as we can – it's *not just ego.*

Getting back to humour: one of my favourites, as well as the Pythons, is *Faulty Towers* . Only twelve episodes were made but they are ageless and always have me in stitches. Michael McIntyre and his *Roadshow* is great fun too. Unlike many modern comics, he doesn't have to use the 'f' word to get a laugh. To me that's real comic skill. We're loving Ricky Gervais with his new series, '*After Life.*' It is comic genius. Trying hard to come to terms with the early death of his wife from cancer, he develops his own way of dealing with his grief whilst interacting with some of the most wonderful TV character actors we've seen for a while. The common man (and woman) become real heroes in the show – great viewing. In the episodes, he can pick an 'arsehole' so easily and gives them heaps. It's really good fun but a bit of pathos too.

So it's back to this beautiful blue ball spinning at 1,040 mph (1,675 km/h) and the mystery of it all. Radio telescopes have been putting messages into space for over fifty years and we've had nothing back! Maybe this is it: we *are* the only planet with life. What about evolution? I'm still waiting for the palaeontologist to find the bones of a giraffe with a shorter neck – evidence that he was struggling to stretch his neck to get to the leaves up the top of a tree. Some of those frightening creatures we see lurking in the great depths of the oceans seem to live such awful lives – what would want to evolve into that, for christ's sake? Life is so interesting and diverse on our planet it's not too difficult to think that a Creator started it all and then maybe left things to evolve. Maybe reincarnation is part of that too? We evolve through various incarnations to finally realise the meaning of life? Sounds like hard work but could be fun. We don't seem to learn too much in the one life, do we? Sometimes we forget that the 'Big Bang' and evolution, as well as creation are still only theories. We do know that the universe is expanding as we can measure it – but why is it expanding? What for? It's all still a mystery, thank god (excuse the pun!).

The law of Karma (cause and effect) is certainly true and we do 'reap what we sow' as I know from personal experience.

If dear old Albert Facey reckons he had a fortunate life (a really good book, by the way) then I reckon I've had a very lucky life as a boomer – and Australia has been good to me.

Anyway, I'd love to finish with a quote from the Pythons' Galaxy Song (Eric Idle in his *'Sortabiography'* says, laughingly, that he argued with Professor Brian Cox about the scientific facts in the song but Eric wins by saying that the facts were right in 1982 when he wrote the lyrics. Who cares – it's brilliant!

"So remember when you're feeling small and insecure,
How amazingly unlikely is your birth;
And pray that there's intelligent life somewhere out in space,
'Cause there's bugger all down here on Earth!"

And – of course! *"Always look on the bright side of life!"* (and death) – from *The Life of Brian*.

THE END
(or a beginning?)

Some of my favourite reads

- Lawrence in Arabia – Scott Anderson
- A Fortunate Life – A.B. Facey
- Desperate Voyage – John Caldwell
- Sailing Alone Round the World – Joshua Slocum
- Cloudstreet – Tim Winton
- Blind Faith – Ben Elton
- The Bible
- Eric Idle – a sortabiography
- People Who Eat Darkness – Richard Parry
- The Outsider – Colin Wilson
- The Poetry and Prose of William Blake
- Selected Poems of T.S. Eliot
- Pride and Prejudice – Jane Austin
- South Sea Vagabonds – J.M. Wray
- Dolphins at Sunset – Elizabeth Thurston
- Apeirogon – Colum McCallum
- The Battle of Britain: Myth and Reality – Richard Overy
- God, Guns and Israel – Jill Hamilton
- Initiation – Elizabeth Haitch

By the same author:

'Lotus 11 - an Indian Ocean Adventure,'
Access Press (1992)

About the Author

Nigel was born in Somerset, UK, and was a child of her Majesty's services; moving around England, Germany and Jordan. He attended two boarding schools. His early working life was mainly as an unskilled worker, trying many jobs. He emigrated to Australia in 1966 as a 'Ten Pound Pom,' arriving in WA after working in Queensland.

Nigel eventually became a West Australian primary teacher for twenty-one years, then a high school relief teacher, while all his adult life he also played music part time.

He married a 4th generation West Australian lady, Aileen, in 1991. They are very happy. Nigel has always sailed since high school in Germany, and has had many adventures, both overseas and around the coast of Australia.

He still plays music with Perth jazz bands and the cabaret band, *The Haze Showband*. Since retiring he has become an RVGA guide, a guide on the *Duyfken* replica, and an active member of U3A. He's always had a passion for writing and wrote, *Lotus 11 – an Indian Ocean Adventure* in 1992. He wrote for '*Cruising Helmsman*' magazine for twenty years. He is a popular guest speaker for Probus and U3A.

www.ingramcontent.com/pod-product-compliance
Lightning Source LLC
Chambersburg PA
CBHW041957080526
44588CB00021B/2775